NES Spanish
401 Teacher Certification Exam

By: Sharon Wynne, M.S.

XAMonline, INC.
Boston

Copyright © 2011 XAMonline, Inc.
All rights reserved. No part of the material protected by this copyright notice may be reproduced or utilized in any form or by any means, electronic or mechanical, including photocopying, recording or by any information storage and retrievable system, without written permission from the copyright holder.

To obtain permission(s) to use the material from this work for any purpose including workshops or seminars, please submit a written request to:

XAMonline, Inc.
25 First Street, Suite 106
Cambridge, MA 02141
Toll Free: 1-800-509-4128
Email: info@xamonline.com
Web: www.xamonline.com
Fax: 1-617-583-5552

Library of Congress Cataloging-in-Publication Data

Wynne, Sharon A.
    NES Spanish 401: Teacher Certification / Sharon A. Wynne. -1st ed.
    ISBN 978-1-60787-088-3
    1. NES Spanish 401   2. Study Guides.   3. NES
    4. Teachers' Certification & Licensure.   5. Careers

Disclaimer:

The opinions expressed in this publication are the sole works of XAMonline and were created independently from the National Education Association, Educational Testing Service, or any State Department of Education, National Evaluation Systems or other testing affiliates.

Between the time of publication and printing, state specific standards as well as testing formats and website information may change that is not included in part or in whole within this product. Sample test questions are developed by XAMonline and reflect similar content as on real tests; however, they are not former tests. XAMonline assembles content that aligns with state standards but makes no claims nor guarantees teacher candidates a passing score. Numerical scores are determined by testing companies such as NES or ETS and then are compared with individual state standards. A passing score varies from state to state.

Printed in the United States of America

NES Spanish 401
ISBN: 978-1-60787-088-3

TEACHER CERTIFICATION STUDY GUIDE

TABLE OF CONTENTS

SPANISH – CONTENT KNOWLEDGE

I. Interpretive Listening 1

II. Structure of the Language 13

III. Interpretive Reading 50

IV. Cultural Perspectives 70

SPANISH – PEDAGOGY

I. Planning 117

II. Teaching 121

III. Evaluating Instruction 125

Bibliography 128

Tables – Grammar 130

Maps 143

Sample Test 146

Answer Key 180

Rigor Table 181

Rationales with Sample Questions 182

TEACHER CERTIFICATION STUDY GUIDE

Section 1

About XAMonline

XAMonline – A Specialty Teacher Certification Company
Created in 1996, XAMonline was the first company to publish study guides for state-specific teacher certification examinations. Founder Sharon Wynne found it frustrating that materials were not available for teacher certification preparation and decided to create the first single, state-specific guide. XAMonline has grown into a company of over 1800 contributors and writers and offers over 300 titles for the entire PRAXIS series and every state examination. No matter what state you plan on teaching in, XAMonline has a unique teacher certification study guide just for you.

XAMonline – Value and Innovation
We are committed to providing value and innovation. Our print-on-demand technology allows us to be the first in the market to reflect changes in test standards and user feedback as they occur. Our guides are written by experienced teachers who are experts in their fields. And, our content reflects the highest standards of quality. Comprehensive practice tests with varied levels of rigor means that your study experience will closely match the actual in-test experience.

To date, XAMonline has helped nearly 600,000 teachers pass their certification or licensing exams. Our commitment to preparation exceeds simply providing the proper material for study - it extends to helping teachers **gain mastery** of the subject matter, giving them the **tools** to become the most effective classroom leaders possible, and ushering today's students toward a **successful future**.

Section 2

About this Study Guide

Purpose of this Guide
Is there a little voice inside of you saying, "Am I ready?" Our goal is to replace that little voice and remove all doubt with a new voice that says, "I AM READY. **Bring it on!**" by offering the highest quality of teacher certification study guides.

Organization of Content
You will see that while every test may start with overlapping general topics, each are very unique in the skills they wish to test. Only XAMonline presents custom content that analyzes deeper than a title or a subarea. Only XAMonline presents content and sample test questions along with the deepest-level rationale and interpretation that are unique to the exam.

How do We Compare with Our Competitors?
XAMonline – drills down to the focus statement level
CliffsNotes and REA – organized at the objective level
Kaplan – provides only links to content
MoMedia – content not specific to the test

Each subarea is divided into manageable sections that cover the specific skill areas. Explanations are easy-to-understand and thorough. You'll find that every test answer contains a rejoinder so if you need a refresher or further review after taking the test, you'll know exactly to which section you must return.

TEACHER CERTIFICATION STUDY GUIDE

How to Use this Book

Our informal polls show that most people begin studying up to 8 weeks prior to the test date, so start early. Then ask yourself some questions: How much do you really know? Are you coming to the test straight from your teacher-education program or are you having to review subjects you haven't considered in 10 years? Either way, take a **diagnostic or assessment test** first. Also, spend time on sample tests so that you become accustomed to the way the actual test will appear.

This guide comes with an online diagnostic test of 30 questions found online at www.XAMonline.com. It is a little boot camp to get you up for the task and reveal things about your compendium of knowledge in general. Although this guide is structured to follow the order of the test, you are not required to study in that order. By finding a time-management and study plan that fits your life you will be more effective. The results of your diagnostic or self-assessment test can be a guide for how to manage your time and point you towards an area that needs more attention.

After taking the diagnostic exam, fill out the **Personalized Study Plan** page at the beginning of each chapter. Review the competencies and skills covered in that chapter and check the boxes that apply to your study needs. If there are sections you already know you can skip, check the "skip it" box. Taking this step will give you a study plan for each chapter.

Week	Activity
8 weeks prior to test	Take a diagnostic test found at www.XAMonline.com
7 weeks prior to test	Build your Personalized Study Plan for each chapter. Check the "skip it" box for sections you feel you are already strong in.
6-3 weeks prior to test	For each of these 4 weeks, choose a content area to study. You don't have to go in the order of the book. It may be that you start with the content that needs the most review. Alternately, you may want to ease yourself into plan by starting with the most familiar material.
2 weeks prior to test	Take the sample test, score it, and create a review plan for the final week before the test.
1 week prior to test	Following your plan (which will likely be aligned with the areas that need the most review) go back and study the sections that align with the questions you may have gotten wrong. Then go back and study the sections related to the questions you answered correctly. If need be, create flashcards and drill yourself on any area that you makes you anxious.

Section 3

About the NES Spanish Exam

What is the NES Spanish Exam?
The NES Spanish exam is designed to ensure that certified teachers wishing to provide Spanish instruction in Oregon public schools possess the requisite knowledge and skills to teach this subject. The exam is aligned to professionally accepted national learning standards.

Often **your own state's requirements** determine whether or not you should take any particular test. The most reliable source of information regarding this is your state's Department of Education. This resource should have a complete list of testing centers and dates. Test dates vary by subject area and not all test dates necessarily include your particular test, so be sure to check carefully.

If you are in a teacher-education program, check with the Education Department or the Certification Officer for specific information for testing and testing timelines. The Certification Office should have most of the information you need.

If you choose an alternative route to certification you can either rely on our website at www.XAMonline.com or on the resources provided by an alternative certification program. Many states now have specific agencies devoted to alternative certification and there are some national organizations as well, for example:
National Association for Alternative Certification
http://www.alt-teachercert.org/index.asp

TEACHER CERTIFICATION STUDY GUIDE

Interpreting Test Results

Contrary to what you may have heard, the results of the NES Spanish test are not based on time. More accurately, you will be scored on the raw number of points you earn in relation to the raw number of points available. Each question is worth one raw point. It is likely to your benefit to complete as many questions in the time allotted, but it will not necessarily work to your advantage if you hurry through the test.

The passing score for the NES Spanish exam is 226.

Follow the guidelines provided by Pearson Education, Inc. for interpreting your score. The web site offers a sample test score sheet and clearly explains how/whether the scores are scaled and what to expect if you have an essay portion on your test. Scores are available by mail two weeks after the test date and scores will be sent to you and your chosen institution(s).

What's on the Test?

The NES Spanish 401 exam lasts 3 hours and consists of 100 multiple-choice questions, 1 presentational writing task, and 1 presentation speaking task.

The breakdown of the questions is as follows:

Section	Approximate Number of Questions	Approximate Percentage of the Test	Time (in minutes)
Interpretative Listening	26	15%	27 (approximate)
Interpretative Reading	26	15%	27 (suggested)
Language Structures	22	13%	23 (suggested)
Cultural Understanding	26	15%	27 (suggested)
Presentational Writing	1	20%	36 suggested
Presentational Speaking	1	22%	40 suggested

TEACHER CERTIFICATION STUDY GUIDE

Question Types

You're probably thinking, enough already, I want to study! Indulge us a little longer while we explain that there is actually more than one type of multiple-choice question. You can thank us later after you realize how well prepared you are for your exam.

1. **Complete the Statement.** The name says it all. In this question type you'll be asked to choose the correct completion of a given statement. For example: The Dolch Basic Sight Words consist of a relatively short list of words that children should be able to:

    a. Sound out
    b. Know the meaning of
    c. Recognize on sight
    d. Use in a sentence

    The correct answer is C. In order to check your answer, test out the statement by adding the choices to the end of it.

2. **Which of the Following.** One way to test your answer choice for this type of question is to replace the phrase "which of the following" with your selection. Use this example: Which of the following words is one of the twelve most frequently used in children's reading texts:

    a. There
    b. This
    c. The
    d. An

    Don't look! Test your answer. ____ is one of the twelve most frequently used in children's reading texts. Did you guess C? Then you guessed correctly.

TEACHER CERTIFICATION STUDY GUIDE

3. **Roman Numeral Choices.** This question type is used when there is more than one possible correct answer. For example: Which of the following two arguments accurately supports the use of cooperative learning as an effective method of instruction?

    I. Cooperative learning groups facilitate healthy competition between individuals in the group.
    II. Cooperative learning groups allow academic achievers to carry or cover for academic underachievers.
    III. Cooperative learning groups make each student in the group accountable for the success of the group.
    IV. Cooperative learning groups make it possible for students to reward other group members for achieving.

    A. I and II
    B. II and III
    C. I and III
    D. III and IV

    Notice that the question states there are **two** possible answers. It's best to read all the possibilities first before looking at the answer choices. In this case, the correct answer is D.

4. **Negative Questions.** This type of question contains words such as "not," "least," and "except." Each correct answer will be the statement that does **not** fit the situation described in the question. Such as: Multicultural education is **not**

    a. An idea or concept
    b. A "tack-on" to the school curriculum
    c. An educational reform movement
    d. A process

    Think to yourself that the statement could be anything but the correct answer. This question form is more open to interpretation than other types, so read carefully and don't forget that you're answering a negative statement.

5. **Questions That Include Graphs, Tables, or Reading Passages.** As ever, read the question carefully. It likely asks for a very specific answer and not broad interpretation of the visual. Here is a simple (though not statistically accurate) example of a graph question: In the following graph in how many years did more men take the NYSTCE exam than women?

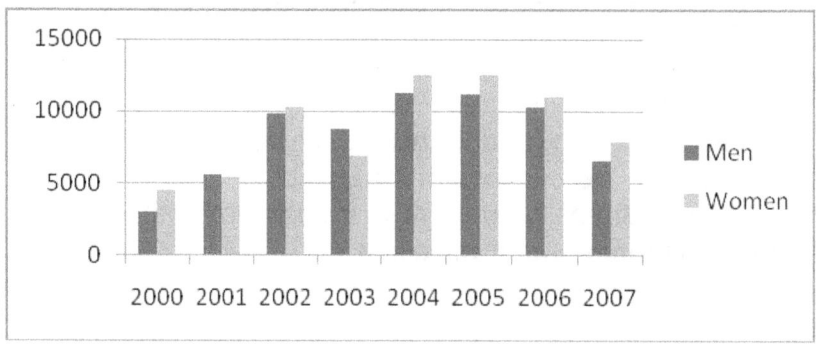

   a. None
   b. One
   c. Two
   d. Three

It may help you to simply circle the two years that answer the question. Make sure you've read the question thoroughly and once you've made your determination, double check your work. The correct answer is C.

Section 4

Helpful Hints

Study Tips

1. **You are what you eat.** Certain foods aid the learning process by releasing natural memory enhancers called CCKs (cholecystokinin) composed of tryptophan, choline, and phenylalanine. All of these chemicals enhance the neurotransmitters associated with memory and certain foods release memory enhancing chemicals. A light meal or snacks from the following foods fall into this category:
    - Milk
    - Nuts and seeds
    - Rice
    - Oats
    - Eggs
    - Turkey
    - Fish

   The better the connections, the more you comprehend!

2. **See the forest for the trees.** In other words, get the concept before you look at the details. One way to do this is to take notes as you read, paraphrasing or summarizing in your own words. Putting the concept in terms that are comfortable and familiar may increase retention.

3. **Question authority.** Ask why, why, why. Pull apart written material paragraph by paragraph and don't forget the captions under the illustrations. For example, if a heading reads *Stream Erosion* put it in the form of a question (why do streams erode? Or what is stream erosion?) then find the answer within the material. If you train your mind to think in this manner you will learn more and prepare yourself for answering test questions.

4. **Play mind games**. Using your brain for reading or puzzles keeps it flexible. Even with a limited amount of time your brain can take in data (much like a computer) and store it for later use. In ten minutes you can: read two paragraphs (at least), quiz yourself with flash cards, or review notes. Even if you don't fully understand something on the first pass, your mind stores it for recall, which is why frequent reading or review increases chances of retention and comprehension.

5. **The pen is mightier than the sword.** Learn to take great notes. A by-product of our modern culture is that we have grown accustomed to getting our information in short doses. We've subconsciously trained ourselves to assimilate information into neat little packages. Messy notes fragment the flow of information. Your notes can be much clearer with proper formatting. *The Cornell Method* is one such format. This method was popularized in *How to Study in College,* Ninth Edition, by Walter Pauk. You can benefit from the method without purchasing an additional book by simply looking the method up online. Below is a sample of how *The Cornell Method* can be adapted for use with this guide.

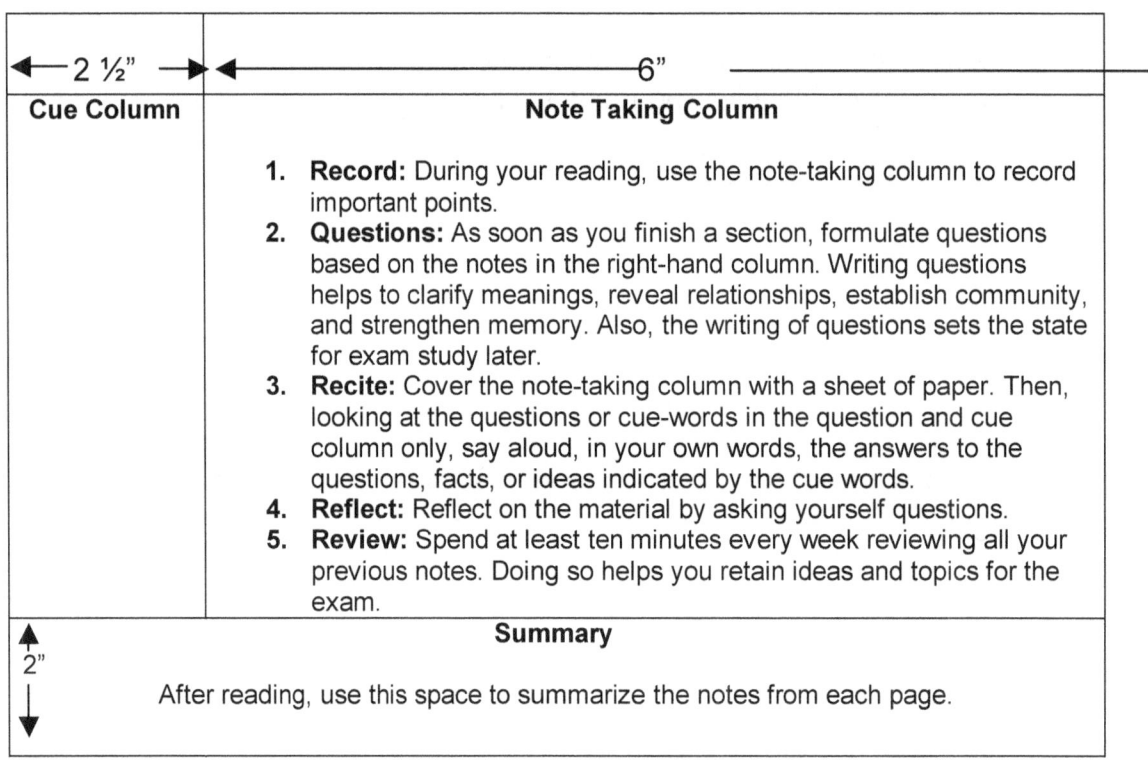

*Adapted from *How to Study in College,* Ninth Edition, by Walter Pauk, ©2008 Wadsworth

6. **Place yourself in exile and set the mood.** Set aside a particular place and time to study that best suits your personal needs and biorhythms. If you're a night person, burn the midnight oil. If you're a morning person set yourself up with some coffee and get to it. Make your study time and place as free from distraction as possible and surround yourself with what you need, be it silence or music. Studies have shown that music can aid in concentration, absorption, and retrieval of information. Not all music, though. Classical music is said to work best.

7. **Get pointed in the right direction.** Use arrows to point to important passages or pieces of information. It's easier to read than a page full of yellow highlights. Highlighting can be used sparingly, but add an arrow to the margin to call attention to it.

8. **Check your budget.** You should at least review all the content material before your test, but allocate the most amount of time to the areas that need the most refreshing. It sounds obvious, but it's easy to forget. You can use the study rubric above to balance your study budget.

> The proctor will write the start time where it can be seen and then, later, provide the time remaining, typically 15 minutes before the end of the test.

TEACHER CERTIFICATION STUDY GUIDE

Testing Tips

1. **Get smart, play dumb.** Sometimes a question is just a question. No one is out to trick you, so don't assume that the test writer is looking for something other than what was asked. Stick to the question as written and don't overanalyze.

2. **Do a double take.** Read test questions and answer choices at least twice because it's easy to miss something, to transpose a word or some letters. If you have no idea what the correct answer is, skip it and come back later if there's time. If you're still clueless, it's okay to guess. Remember, you're scored on the number of questions you answer correctly and you're not penalized for wrong answers. The worst case scenario is that you miss a point from a good guess.

3. **Turn it on its ear.** The syntax of a question can often provide a clue, so make things interesting and turn the question into a statement to see if it changes the meaning or relates better (or worse) to the answer choices.

4. **Get out your magnifying glass.** Look for hidden clues in the questions because it's difficult to write a multiple-choice question without giving away part of the answer in the options presented. In most questions you can readily eliminate one or two potential answers, increasing your chances of answering correctly to 50/50, which will help out if you've skipped a question and gone back to it (see tip #2).

5. **Call it intuition.** Often your first instinct is correct. If you've been studying the content you've likely absorbed something and have subconsciously retained the knowledge. On questions you're not sure about trust your instincts because a first impression is usually correct.

6. **Graffiti.** Sometimes it's a good idea to mark your answers directly on the test booklet and go back to fill in the optical scan sheet later. You don't get extra points for perfectly blackened ovals. If you choose to manage your test this way, be sure not to mismark your answers when you transcribe to the scan sheet.

7. **Become a clock-watcher.** You have a set amount of time to answer the questions. Don't get bogged down laboring over a question you're not sure about when there are ten others you could answer more readily. If you choose to follow the advice of tip #6, be sure you leave time near the end to go back and fill in the scan sheet.

TEACHER CERTIFICATION STUDY GUIDE

Do the Drill

No matter how prepared you feel it's sometimes a good idea to apply Murphy's Law. So the following tips might seem silly, mundane, or obvious, but we're including them anyway.

1. **Remember, you are what you eat, so bring a snack.** Choose from the list of energizing foods that appear earlier in the introduction.

2. **You're not too sexy for your test.** Wear comfortable clothes. You'll be distracted if your belt is too tight, or if you're too cold or too hot.

3. **Lie to yourself.** Even if you think you're a prompt person, pretend you're not and leave plenty of time to get to the testing center. Map it out ahead of time and do a dry run if you have to. There's no need to add road rage to your list of anxieties.

4. **Bring sharp, number 2 pencils.** It may seem impossible to forget this need from your school days, but you might. And make sure the erasers are intact, too.

5. **No ticket, no test.** Bring your admission ticket as well as **two** forms of identification, including one with a picture and signature. You will not be admitted to the test without these things.

6. **You can't take it with you.** Leave any study aids, dictionaries, notebooks, computers and the like at home. Certain tests **do** allow a scientific or four-function calculator, so check ahead of time if your test does.

7. **Prepare for the desert.** Any time spent on a bathroom break **cannot** be made up later, so use your judgment on the amount you eat or drink.

8. **Quiet, Please!** Keeping your own time is a good idea, but not with a timepiece that has a loud ticker. If you use a watch, take it off and place it nearby but not so that it distracts you. And **silence your cell phone.**

To the best of our ability, we have compiled the content you need to know in this book and in the accompanying online resources. The rest is up to you. You can use the study and testing tips or you can follow your own methods. Either way, you can be confident that there aren't any missing pieces of information and there shouldn't be any surprises in the content on the test.

If you have questions about test fees, registration, electronic testing, or other content verification issues please visit www.ets.org

Good luck!
Sharon Wynne
Founder, XAMonline

TEACHER CERTIFICATION STUDY GUIDE

I. INTERPRETIVE LISTENING

Sound Discrimination

Letter	Sound	Usage	Similar Eng. Sound	Examples
B, V	[b]	beginning of word or after consonant	boy	bien árbol vosotros invierno
	bilabial fricative	everywhere else	n/a	hablar problema nueve noventa
C	[th]	preceding E or I		once diciembre
	[k]	preceding A, O, U, or consonant		como cuatro octubre
D	[d]	beginning of word or after L or N	dog had	dos cuándo falda
	[TH]	everywhere else	this bathe	adiós perdón salud
G	[g]	preceding A, O, U, or consonant	gave go gum glow	agosto agua galleta grande
	[kh]	preceding E or I	ch in loch	gente gigante

S	[z]	preceding B, D, G, L, M, N	rose cause	mismo desde
	[s]	everywhere else	house some	escuela gris sombrero
X	[ks]	n/a	axe mix	éxito except
	[gz]	n/a	exact	exacto exigir

Word Discrimination

For this section, see word list on pages 4 and 5.

1. Él funda su propia organización con el deseo de ganar plata.
2. Cuando él lee, se le encienden los ojos.
3. Ayer casi cojo al hombre cojo que se cayó de sus muletas.
4. Él botó el voto.
5. Como ves, todos se fueron de una vez.
6. Llena la funda con pollo.
7. Si usted calla al comediante, yo lo apoyo.
8. Cuando él prendió la luz, todo fue diferente.

1. *He establishes his own organization with the purpose of making money.*
2. *When he reads, his eyes turn on.*
3. *Yesterday I almost grabbed the injured man who fell off his crutches.*
4. *He threw out the vote.*
5. *Don't you see, they all left at once.*
6. *Fill the bag with chicken.*
7. *If it was you who made the comedian shut up, I'll support you.*
8. *When he lit the light, all was different.*

Meaning of Words in Spanish

Synonyms/Antonyms

Synonyms			
dormir / descansar	estudiar / aprender	comer / alimentar	casa / residencia
sleep / rest	study / learn	eat / feed	house / residence

Antonyms			
paz / guerra	dormir / despertar	muerte / vida	descansar / trabajar
peace / war	sleep / awake	death / life	rest / work

Changes caused by minimal modification

gente / lente	gracias / gracia	río / rio
people / lens	thank you / grace	river / laugh
casa / caza	café / café	vino / vino
house / hunt	coffee / brown	came (he-she) / wine
calle / calle	cojo / cojo	lee / le
street / be quiet	grab / limp-injured	read / him-her
cuenta / cuenta	miente / mente	voto / botó
count / bead	lies (he – she) / mind	vote / threw out
funda / funda	callo / calló / cayó	apoyo / pollo
bag, sheet / establishes (he-she)	callus / became quiet / fell	support / chicken
ves / vez	pasa / pasa	luz / luz
see (you) / again-time	pass / happens	light / lamp

Meaning of Sentences in Spanish

Rigoberta Menchú, una indígena Guatemalteca que nació en 1959, ganó el Premio Nóbel de la Paz en 1992. Viajará a varios países, entre ellos, España. Menchú va a estar en Madrid donde dialogará con el nuevo presidente del gobierno español. Menchú va a discutir las maneras en que sufre la población indígena de América Latina. Rigoberta Menchú ha dedicado sus esfuerzos y trabajo de vida a este grupo.

¿Cuál es el propósito del viaje de Rigoberta Menchú a España?

A. Viajar a varios países europeos

B. Conocer personalmente al Príncipe Felipe de Borbón

C. Recibir el Premio Nóbel de la Paz

D. Hablar sobre sus esfuerzos por las comunidades indígenas. (correcta)

El Príncipe Felipe de Borbón, el futuro líder de España, nació en 1968. Estudió en Canadá y en Estados Unidos. Es muy atlético y se interesa mucho en los deportes. Aunque el príncipe es famoso lleva una vida bastante normal. Está bien preparado para ser el próximo Rey de España, según los políticos europeos.

¿Qué se destaca en este texto que le gusta al Príncipe Felipe?

A. Conversar con los norteamericanos

B. Visitar las universidades canadienses

C. Practicar deportes (correcta)

D. Visitar las ciudades norteamericanas

TEACHER CERTIFICATION STUDY GUIDE

Meaning of Passages in Spanish

Federico García Lorca fue un famoso escritor y poeta español de la llamada Generación del 27. Había nacido en Fuente Vaqueros, cerca de Granada, el 5 de junio de 1898. Murió asesinado durante la Guerra Civil Española.

García Lorca estudió filosofía en la ciudad de Córdoba. Luego fue a Madrid a continuar sus estudios. Allí conoció a Pablo Picasso, Salvador Dalí, Manuel de Falla y Andrés Segovia. Viajó a la Argentina, Cuba y los Estados Unidos.

¿Por qué se destacó Federico García Lorca?

A. Por sus poesías (correcta)

B. Por sus esculturas

C. Por sus pinturas

D. Por sus viajes al extranjero

¿Dónde conoció García Lorca a Pablo Picasso, Salvador Dalí, Manuel de Falla y Andrés Segovia?

A. En Argentina

B. En Madrid (correcta)

C. En La Habana

D. En los Estados Unidos

Speaking: Dialogue

Claudio: Hola. ¿Cómo has estado?

Don Fintesco: Perfecto. ¿Qué necesitas?

Claudio: Pues te cuento, tengo mucha plata. Mis negocios van bien. Ahora te voy a proponer una nueva empresa en la cual tú me puedes ayudar. Resulta que en mis viajes conocí una princesa sueca y ella me habló de su amor por las esmeraldas y la falta de aquéllas en su colección personal. Naturalmente le ofrecí mi ayuda.

Don Fintesco: Se pone interesante tu cuento. ¿Cuánto crees que va ella a pagar por la piedra de sus sueños?

Claudio: No es para soñar, sino para vivir, mi apreciado amigo. Ella llega este viernes y tu tarea es de darme a mí, no antes del jueves en la media noche, una piedra de quince quilates.

Don Fintesco: ¿Cómo que estás loco? ¿Dónde voy a encontrar una piedra así en tres días? ¿Adentro de mi zapato?

Claudio: No me importan los detalles, tráela el jueves y te daré cuarenta por ciento de lo que gane en la venta. ¡Hasta entonces, amigo!

¿Cuál es el tema principal de esta conversación?

A. Un cuento de príncipes y princesas

B. Una novela de amor

C. Un negocio de piedras preciosas (correcta)

D. El casamiento de una princesa sueca

¿Quién tiene mucho dinero haciendo negocios?

A. Claudio (correcta)

B. Don Fintesco

C. La princesa sueca

D. Los dos amigos

Conversación entre dos vehículos, un viejo camión americano y un moderno automóvil japonés

Camión viejo americano: - AME

Automóvil moderno japonés: JAP

AME: - ¡Hola! ¿Por qué sonríes tanto? Parece que eres muy orgulloso.

JAP: - ¡Mira! Por supuesto que estoy orgulloso. Toda la gente de la ciudad me busca. Todos quieren comprar automóviles japoneses como yo.

AME: - Bueno, eso es cierto, pero en parte. La gente que piensa poco compra para hoy, pero no para mañana.

JAP: - ¿Qué dices? ¿Estás ciego? ¿Quién paga acaso $1000 por ti? Tú ya no sirves.

AME: ¡Mira, no ofendas! Se conoce que sabes poco de los Estados Unidos. Aquí en la ciudad pocos me miran. Pero en la montaña, en el campo, en la pradera todos me buscan, pues todos saben que yo sigo caminando y seguiré caminando cuando tú estés en el cementerio.

JAP: No lo creo. Los japoneses les superamos en tecnología.

AME: Probablemente sí, si hablas de un camión Chevrolet del 50 como yo, pero cualquier mecánico de cualquier pueblo de aquí y de cualquier parte del mundo sabe solucionar mis problemas. A ti te tienen que llevar a Tokio y muchas veces hasta los más expertos no encuentran tus chips quemados.

JAP: Parece que contigo no se puede hablar porque siempre tienes una respuesta.
AME: Yo soy lo mejor en cuanto a mecánica y además no le causo serios problemas a nadie. Siempre sigo adelante aunque tenga alguna batería muy gastada o mis bujías estén sucias.

¿Por qué el viejo camión siempre va hacia adelante?

A) Porque no es japonés

B) Porque consume poca gasolina

C) Porque cuesta sólo $1000

D) Porque su mecánica es simple y segura (correcta)

Spoken Information from Daily-life Sources

Buenos días señor. Nos ponemos en contacto con usted con motivo de su reciente visita a nuestra agencia de viajes, donde mencionó su interés por viajar este fin de semana a la Isla Paraíso con un plan no muy costoso que se adecúe a sus posibilidades. Con su permiso lo podría incluir en nuestro plan de costos rebajados y así, rápidamente, entregarle su boleta para su próximo destino.

Good morning, Sir. We are calling you due to your visit to our travel agency, where you showed interest to visit Paradise Isle this weekend with an inexpensive plan according to your possibilities. Could we include you in our low cost plan to immediately issue your ticket for the next destination?

¿Cuál es le motivo de la llamada de la agencia de viajes?

A. Ofrecer un costoso plan de turismo a la Isla Paraíso

B. Ofrecer un plan de costos rebajados para la Isla Paraíso (correcta)

C. Ofrecer un plan de viajes a otros sitios turísticos

D. Pedir disculpas por no tener planes disponibles

*   *   *

Para usar Shampoo Grow!:

"Simplemente moje su cabello, dé un masaje en todo su pelo, y déjeselo por 3 minutos y luego enjuague. Puede dar una segunda pasada, si usted gusta, pero Grow! hace el trabajo de una vez. Al mismo tiempo, Grow! contiene ingredientes delicados que le permiten que se use a diario, y así usted no necesita estar alternando con otros shampoos."

To use Grow! Shampoo:

"Simply wet your hair, massage it onto all your hair and leave for three minutes and then rinse. Can be given a second time over, if you like, but Grow! does the work at once. At the same time, Grow! contains delicate ingredients that permit daily use for you and that way, you don't need to be alternating with other shampoos."

¿Qué se dice sobre Grow! Shampoo?

A. Es un shampoo para mujeres y niños.

B. Es un shampoo para hombres.

C. Cómo usar este shampoo a diario. (correcta)

D. Cuáles son los peligros de usarlo a diario.

II. STRUCTURE OF THE LANGUAGE

Structures and Usage of the Present Indicative and the Infinitive in Spanish

Present Indicative

Use of the present indicative tense:

- to refer to the here and now
- to refer to an immediate future
- to refer to an historical past (*hace* + an expression of time _ *que* + verb in the present indicative)

Dropping the infinitive ending and adding the following endings form the present indicative of regular verbs:

-ar verbs (-o, -as, -a, -amos, -áis, -an)
-er verbs (-o, -es, -e, -emos, -éis, -en)
-ir verbs (-o, -es, -e, -imos, -ís, -en)

- -ar verbs: The present indicative of stem changing verbs that end in –ar is as follows:

    Example: Pensar (pienso, piensas, piensa, pensamos, pensáis, piensan)

Other stem changing verbs conjugated like "pensar" are:

acertar, apretar, atravesar, cerrar, comenzar, confesar, despertar, empezar, encerrar, gobernar, helar, nevar, quebrar, remendar, sentar

    Example: Mostrar (muestro, muestras, muestra, mostramos, mostráis, muestran)

Other stem changing verbs conjugated like "mostrar" are:

acordar, acostar, almorzar, contar, costar, encontrar, jugar ("u" to "ue"), recordar, renovar, tronar, volar

- -er verbs: The present indicative of stem changing verbs that end in –er is as follows:

    Example: Querer (quiero, quieres, quiere, queremos, queréis, quieren)

Other stem changing verbs conjugated like "querer" are:

    ascender, defender, descender, encender, entender, perder

    Example: Volver (vuelvo, vuelves, vuelve, volvemos, volvéis, vuelven)

Other stem changing verbs that end in –er are:

    conmover, devolver, doler, llover, mover, oler ("o" to "hue"), poder, resolver, soler

- -ir verbs: The present indicative of stem changing verbs that end in –ir is as follows:

    Example: Consentir (consiento, consientes, consiente, consentimos, consentís, consienten)

Other stem changing verbs conjugated like "consentir" are:

    advertir, convertir, divertir, hervir, mentir, preferir, referir, sentir

    Example: Dormir (duermo, duermes, duerme, dormimos, dormís, duermen)

Another stem changing verb conjugated like "dormir" is "morir."

    Example: Pedir (pido, pides, pide, pedimos, pedís, piden)

Other stem changing verbs conjugated like "pedir" are:

    despedir, gemir, impedir, medir, reír, reñir, repetir, servir, sonreír, vestir

The present indicative of verbs ending in –uir is as follows:

    Example: Huir (huyo, huyes, huye, huimos, huís, huyen)

The present indicative of certain verbs ending in –iar is as follows:

    Example: Enviar (envío, envías, envía, enviamos, enviáis, envían)

Other verbs conjugated like "enviar" are "confiar" and "espiar."

Verbs with Irregular Forms in the Present Indicative:

Decir	Estar	Haber	Ir
digo	estoy	he	voy
dices	estás	has	vas
dice	está	ha	va
decimos	estamos	hemos	vamos
decís	estáis	habéis	vais
dicen	están	han	van

Oír	Ser	Tener*	Venir
oigo	soy	tengo	vengo
oyes	eres	tienes	vienes
oye	es	tiene	viene
oímos	somos	tenemos	venimos
oís	sois	tenéis	venís
oyen	son	tienen	vienen

*Also conjugated like "tener" are the following: contener, detener, entretener, mantener, obtener, sostener.

Verbs with Irregular Forms only in the First Person Singular of Present Indicative:

- Caber – yo quepo
- Dar – yo doy
- Hacer – yo hago
- Poner* – yo pongo
- Conocer** – yo conozco
- Saber – yo sé
- Salir – yo salgo
- Coger – yo cojo
- Valer – yo valgo

*Also conjugated like "poner" are the following:

componer, disponer, imponer, oponer, proponer

*Also conjugated like "conocer" are the following:

aborrecer, agradecer, aparecer, carecer, crecer, desaparecer, desconocer, establecer, estremecerse, merecer, nacer, obedecer, ofrecer, parecer, permanecer, pertenecer, reconocer

Spelling Changes in the Present Indicative:

- verbs ending in –cer or –cir: the "c" changes to "z" before adding "o" or "a"
- verbs ending in –ger or –gir: the "g" changes to "j" before adding "o" or "a"
- verbs ending in –guir: the "gu" changes to "g" before adding "o" or "a"

The present indicative of verbs ending in –uar is as follows:

Example: Continuar (continúo, continúas, continúa, continuamos, continuáis, continúan)

Other verbs conjugated like "continuar" are "actuar" and "graduar."

Infinitives are used:

- as the subject of a sentence
- with prepositions
- with present participles
- with passive voice

Structure and Usage of the Preterite and Imperfect Tenses in Spanish

The Preterite Indicative is used:

- to express specific actions or events completed in the past
- to express a specific action or event at a specific point in time
- to state a particular action

The preterite tense of regular verbs is formed by dropping the infinitive ending and adding the following endings:

    -ar verbs (-é, -aste, -ó, -amos, -asteis, -aron)
    -er and -ir verbs (-í, -iste, -ió, -imos, -isteis, -ieron)

Verbs that end in –er and –ir and contain a vowel immediately before the ending change in the third person singular from –ió to –yo

    Examples: caer - cayó, creer – creyó

    Exceptions: traer - trajo, atraer – atrajo

Verbs ending in –car, -gar, and –zar change in the first person singular of the preterite as follows:

    "c" changes to "qu" (example: brincar – yo brinqué)
    "g" changes to "gu" (example: colgar – yo colgué)
    "z" changes to "c" (example: cazar – yo cacé)

Verbs that have a stem change in the present tense also have a stem change in the preterite tense.

The following verbs have an irregular stem in the preterite:

    caber, haber, hacer, poder, poner, querer, saber, tener, venir, decir, producir, traer

The endings for these verbs are –e, -iste, -o, -imos, -isteis, -ieron.

"Hacer" changes to "hizo" in the third person singular.

All compounds of "poner" (example: proponer), "tener," "hacer," "convenir," and "traer" are conjugated in the same manner as the basic verb.

All verbs ending in ducir are conjugated like "producir."

Verbs that are completely irregular in the preterite are the following:
dar: di, diste, dio, dimos, disteis, dieron
ser and ir: fui, fuiste, fue, fuimos, fuisteis, fueron

Verbs with Irregular Forms in the Preterite:

Tener	Estar	Andar	Saber
tuve	estuve	anduve	supe
tuviste	estuviste	anduviste	supiste
tuvo	estuvo	anduvo	supo
tuvimos	estuvimos	anduvimos	supimos
tuvisteis	estuvisteis	anduvisteis	supisteis
tuvieron	estuvieron	anduvieron	supieron

Poner	Poder	Querer	Hacer
puse	pude	quise	hice
pusiste	pudiste	quisiste	hiciste
puso	pudo	quiso	hizo
pusimos	pudimos	quisimos	hicimos
pusisteis	pudisteis	quisisteis	hicisteis
pusieron	pudieron	quisieron	hicieron

Venir	Decir	Traer	Dar
vine	dije	traje	di
viniste	dijiste	trajiste	diste
vino	dijo	trajo	dio
vinimos	dijimos	trajimos	dimos
vinisteis	dijisteis	trajisteis	disteis
vinieron	dijeron	trajeron	dieron

Ver	Ir	Ser
vi	fui	fui
viste	fuiste	fuiste
vio	fue	fue
vimos	fuimos	fuimos
visteis	fuisteis	fuisteis
vieron	fueron	fueron

The Imperfect Tense is used:

- to describe what was happening, used to happen, or happened repeatedly in the past
- to describe persons or things in the past
- to tell a story, set the stage of a story
- to express a state of mind in the past
- to express past numbers, age, temperature, etc.
- to emphasize what was going on in the past when another action took place

The imperfect tense of regular verbs is formed by dropping the infinitive ending and by adding the following endings:

- ar verbs (-aba, -abas, -aba, -ábamos, -abais, -aban)
- er and -ir verbs (-ía, -ías, -ía, -íamos, -ías, -ían)

Verbs Irregular in the Imperfect:

Ser (era, eras, era, éramos, erais, eran)
Ir (iba, ibas, iba, íbamos, ibais, iban)
Ver (veía, veías, veía, veíamos, veíais, veían)

Structure and Usage of Past Participles in Spanish

The past participle of regular verbs is formed by dropping the infinitive ending and adding "-ado" for –ar verbs and "ido" for –er and –ir verbs.

The past participles of –er and –ir verbs with stems ending in a vowel take an accent mark.

Common verbs with irregular past participles include:

abrir	-	abierto
cubrir	-	cubierto
escribir	-	escrito
morir	-	muerto
poner	-	puesto
romper	-	roto
ver	-	visto
volver	-	vuelto
decir	-	dicho
hacer	-	hecho

Present Perfect (Pretérito Perfecto Compuesto)

The present perfect tense is used:

- to describe an action that began in the past and continues up to the present
- to describe an action that took place in the past but is connected with the present

This tense is formed with the present tense of "haber" and the past participle.

    Examples: He estudiado dos horas.
                         Han vivido en esta casa cuatro años.

Structures and Usage of Present Participles in Spanish

Progressive Tenses

The gerund is equivalent to the English present participle and is formed by dropping the infinitive ending and adding the following:

   -ar verbs: ando   -er and –ir verbs: iendo

The gerund of –er and –ir verbs with stems ending in a vowel is formed by adding –yendo.

   Examples: atraer – atrayendo, construir – construyendo

In the gerund, stem changing –ir verbs change the stem vowel from "e" to "i" and from "o" to "u."

   Examples: advertir – advirtiendo, dormir – durmiendo

An irregular gerund is formed changing the infinitive poder to pudiendo.

The gerund is used with forms of the verbs "estar," "seguir," and "continuar."

   Examples: está comiendo, sigue corriendo, continúa hablando.

Structure and Usage of the Future and Conditional Tenses in Spanish

Future

The future tense is used to express a state of being or action that will take place sometime in the future and is used to indicate:

- conjecture regarding the present
- probability regarding the present
- indirect quotations

*The future is never used after *si*, when *si* means "if."

The future tense of regular -ar, -er, and –ir verbs is formed by adding the following endings to the infinitive:

(-é, -ás, -á, -emos, -éis, -án)

Verbs that have accent marks in the infinitive drop that accent in the future.

Verbs like "poder" drop the "e" of the infinitive and then add the endings of the future tense. Other such verbs are "caber," "haber," "querer," and "saber."

Examples: podré, habré, querré, sabré.

In verbs like "poner," the "e" of the infinitive is replaced by a "d" and the endings of the future tense are added. Other such verbs are "salir," "tener," "valer," and "venir."

Examples: pondré, tendré, valdré, vendré.

The verbs "decir" and "hacer" are irregular in the future tense.

Decir: diré, dirás, dirá, diremos, diréis, dirán
Hacer: haré, harás, hará, haremos, haréis, harán

Compounds of the irregular verbs are also irregular.

Example: contradiré

Conditional

The conditional tense is used to express:

- an action that you would do if something else were possible
- a conditional desire while being courteous
- an indirect quotation
- a conjecture regarding the past
- a probability regarding the past

The conditional tense of regular verbs is formed by adding the following endings to the infinitive of -ar, -er, and –ir verbs:

(-ía, -ías, -ía, -íamos, -íais, -ían)

Verbs that have accent marks in the infinitive drop that accent in the conditional.

Example: reír – reiría

Verbs like "poder" drop the "e" of the infinitive and then add the endings of the conditional tense. Other such verbs are "caber," "haber," "querer," and "saber."

Examples: podría, habría, querría, sabría

The verbs "decir" and "hacer" are irregular in the conditional tense.
Decir: diría, dirías, diría, diríamos, diríais, dirían
Hacer: haría, harías, haría, haríamos, haríais, harían

Compounds of the irregular verbs are also irregular. Example: contradiría

Structure and Usage of the Passive Voice and the Impersonal Tense in Spanish

The passive voice in Spanish is formed as follows:

True passive: La flor fue cogida por él.

Or

Reflexive passive: Se cogió la flor.

Other examples:

>Se perdieron los libros.
>Se comieron los mariscos en poco tiempo.

The Subjunctive Mood in Spanish (including present, imperfect, perfect, and pluperfect subjunctive forms)

Subjunctive

The subjunctive mood often clouds the facts, expresses an opinion or emotion, or indirect command. The following mnemonic device might help you to remember some of the uses:

> **W** ish
> **E** motion
> **D** esire
> **D** oubt/denial
> **I** mpersonal expressions
> **N** egation
> **G** eneral commands
> **S** peculation about the future

The present subjunctive is used if the verb in the main clause is present, future, imperative, or perfect.

Dropping the ending "-o" of the first person singular and adding the following endings form the present subjunctive of most verbs:

-ar verbs (-e, -es, - e, emos, - éis, - en)
-er and –ir verbs (-a, -as, -a, -amos, -áis, -an)

In verbs ending in –car, -gar, and –zar change the "c" to "qu," the "g" to "gu" and the "z" to "c."

Examples:
- secar: seque, seques, seque, sequemos...
- rogar: ruegue, ruegues, ruege, roguemos...
- alzar: alce, alces, alce, alcemos…

Stem changing verbs have the same stem changes in the subjunctive as in the present indicative.

Irregular Verbs in the Present Subjunctive

Dar	Estar	Haber	Ir	Saber	Ser
dé	esté	haya	vaya	sepa	sea
des	estés	hayas	vayas	sepas	seas
dé	esté	haya	vaya	sepa	sea
demos	estemos	hayamos	vayamos	sepamos	seamos
deis	estéis	hayáis	vayáis	sepáis	seáis
den	estén	hayan	vayan	sepan	sean

Imperfect Subjunctive

The imperfect subjunctive is used if the verb in the main clause is imperfect, preterite, conditional, or pluperfect.

The imperfect subjunctive of all –ar, -er, -ir verbs is formed by adding the following endings to the verb stem:

-iera / -iese
-ieras / -ieses
-iera / -iese
-iéramos / -iésemos
-ierais / -ieseis
-ieran / -iesen

Examples:

yo	com-iera *or* com-iese
tú	com-ieras *or* com-ieses
él, ella, Ud.	com-iera *or* com-iese
nosotros	com-iéramos *or* com-iésemos
vosotros	com-ierais *or* com-ieseis
ellos, ellas, Uds.	com-ieran *or* com-iesen

Perfect Subjunctive

The perfect subjunctive consists of the present subjunctive of "haber" plus a past participle.

Example: Espero que haya parado de llover para las tres.

Pluperfect Subjunctive

The pluperfect subjunctive consists of the imperfect subjunctive of "haber" plus a past participle.

Example: No esperaba que hubieran llegado tan temprano.

Use present subjunctive or perfect subjunctive if the verb of the main clause is in the following tenses:

- Present indicative
- Present perfect
- Future command

Use imperfect subjunctive or pluperfect subjunctive if the verb in the main clause is in the following tenses:

- Imperfect
- Preterite
- Conditional
- Pluperfect

Reflexive Verbs in Spanish

A verb is used reflexively when the subject of the verb is also its object. When a verb is reflexive, the infinitive ends in "se." Examples of reflexive verbs are:

   Llamarse
   Enjabonarse
   Cortarse
   Acordarse
   Valerse
   Caerse
   Callarse

Reflexive verbs are conjugated by adding the reflexive pronoun before the regular case.

   Examples:

   Yo me llamo Joaquín.

   Si os acordáis de mi cara, decídmelo.

Structure and Usage of Nouns in Spanish

Nouns that end in –a, -dad, -tad, -tud, -umbre, -ie, or –ion are usually feminine.

    Examples: la casa, la humedad, la multitud, la mansedumbre, la perfección.

Nouns that end in –o are usually masculine.

    Examples: el lobo, el cuaderno, el horno.

Nouns that end in a vowel form the plural by adding "s." Those that end in a consonant form the plural by adding –es.

    Examples: silla – sillas, bolígrafo – bolígrafos,
                     sillón – sillones, árbol – árboles.

Nouns ending in –z change the –z to –c before adding –es.

    Examples: pez – peces, audaz – audaces.

Structure and Usage of Articles in Spanish

Definite Articles

Definite articles - as does the English definite article, "the" refers to definite persons or things already mentioned or known about. They are: "el," "la," "los," and "las."

> Singular: "el," m. "la," fem.
> Plural: "los," m. "las," fem.

Definite articles are required in Spanish and are used:

- before all nouns in a general or all-inclusive sense
- before titles and before adjectives preceding proper names, except in direct address (El profesor Ramírez y el señor García vendrán en 10 minutos. – Señora Juana, venga de prisa.)
- to translate as the English definite article "a" or "an" before proper nouns of measure or rate (Me da un kilo de patatas, por favor.)
- before names of languages except directly after "hablar" and after the prepositions "de" and "en" (El francés es una lengua bonita. Mi hijo habla japonés. La eñe es una letra del español.)
- before all geographical names modified by an adjective or adjectival phrase (La Galicia celta forma una parte de España.)

Indefinite Articles

Indefinite articles, like the English indefinite articles "a," "an," "some," are used to mention non-specific persons or things. They are: "un," "una," "unos," "unas."

> Singular: "un," m. "una," fem.
> Plural: "unos," m. "unas," fem.

Indefinite articles are frequently omitted in Spanish in favor of definite articles and subject pronouns. They are used:

- to indicate an indefinite object
- to indicate an indefinite person
- to indicate other members

They are not used:

- before an unmodified noun after a form of "ser" (to be), especially in reference to occupation, religion, affiliation, or social status (normally, if the noun is modified, the article should be used)
- before "otro" (other)
- before "mil" (thousand) and "cien" (hundred)
- in exclamations using "qué" (what)
- after "con" (with) and "sin" (without)
- frequently after forms of "tener," (to have) "comprar," (to buy) "llevar," (to carry) and some other verbs when generically referring to things that people would normally have or use one at a time

Structure and Usage of Adjectives in Spanish

Position and Agreement

Adjectives in Spanish agree in gender and number with the noun they modify. They may precede or follow the noun. As a general rule, they follow the noun, especially in the case of long adjectives, proper adjectives, adjectives used emphatically, or of any adjective which is used to call attention to some individual object, separating it from other more or less similar objects. Numeral adjectives and adjectives of quantity usually precede the noun.

Some adjectives have different meanings, depending on their position. Some of these are "antiguo," "cierto," "grande," "mismo," "nuevo," "pobre," and "simple". Limiting adjectives (numbers, possessive and demonstrative adjectives, adjectives of quantity) usually precede the noun.

Shortened Adjectives

There are several Spanish adjectives that have a shortened form when they precede certain nouns.

The most common shortened adjectives are those that drop the final -o in front of a masculine singular noun.

The following adjectives drop the final –o when used before a masculine singular noun:

- uno
- primero
- tercero
- malo
- bueno
- ninguno (becomes "ningún") before masculine nouns
- alguno (becomes "algún") before masculine nouns

"Grande" becomes "gran" when used before a singular noun of either gender.

"Ciento" becomes "cien" when used before a noun of either gender and when multiplying numerical quantities.

"Cualquiera" becomes "cualquier" when used before a noun of either gender.

The adjective "Santo" is shortened to "San" when preceding most masculine saints' names.

Comparative Degree

When comparing the quality of two nouns, the adjective is in the comparative degree. The words "más" and "menos" do not change with gender or number.

The comparative degree may express superiority (greater than) using the construction "más" + adjective/adverb + "que" . . .

The comparative degree may express inferiority (less than) using the construction "menos" + adjective/adverb + "que" . . .

The comparative degree may express equality using the construction "tan " + adjective/adverb + "como" . . .

The words "más" and "menos" are not used with the irregular comparatives "mayor" and "peor".

Superlative Degree

The superlative degree of adjectives or adverbs is formed by putting the definite article or a possessive pronoun before the comparative. There are some constructions where simply "más," without the definite article is used, as in the formation of adverbial superlatives.

Words such as "mejor" (best) and "peor" (worst) can also stand alone as superlatives.

With the irregular superlatives, the definite article is used.

Absolute superlatives are also formed by adding the suffix –"ísimo" (-a, -os, -as) to an adjective or an adverb.

- Singular: "ísimo" m.   -"ísima" fem.
- Plural: "ísimos" m.   -"ísimas" fem.

Demonstrative Adjectives

Demonstrative adjectives are words which indicate a specific noun.

                Masculine   **Feminine**

Singular	este	ese	aquel		esta	esa	aquella
Plural	estos	esos	aquellos		estas	esas	aquellas

- this: este, esta
- that: ese, esa, aquel, aquella
- these: estos, estas
- those: esos, esas, aquellos, aquellas

Structure and Usage of Adverbs in Spanish

Adverbs are words that modify a verb, an adjective, or another adverb

Adverbs modify verbs or adjectives to describe how an action (verb) is performed, how intense a quality (adjective) is, etc.:

Habla bien.	She speaks well. (adverb 'well' modifies verb 'speak')
No trabajamos demasiado.	We do not work too much.
Es bastante fácil.	It's quite difficult. (adverb 'quite' modifies adj. 'easy')

Adverbs have no feminine or plural forms.

Son bastante difíciles.	They're quite difficult.
Las flores están demasiado marchitas.	The flowers are too old.
Me gustan mucho las palomitas.	I like popcorn a lot.

Some adverbs, however, function also as adjectives, so they must agree with the noun in number and gender:

Tiene muchos problemas, bastantes preocupaciones y demasiadas deudas.

Adverbs can provide additional information about manner, quantity, frequency, time, or place. Many adverbs are formed from adjectives, by adding the suffix -mente to the feminine singular form, the same way we add (-ly) to an adjective in English. Adverbs explain when, how, where, how often, or to what degree something is done.

Generally, the feminine, singular form of the adjective is the same as the "regular" or masculine, singular form unless the adjective ends in an "o," in which case the -o is changed to an -a.

Examples:

- especialmente (adjective: "especial")
- claramente (adjective: "claro")

Some adverbs do not follow any pattern of origination, and must simply be memorized, such as "muy," "nunca," "mal," or "siempre."

Categories of Adverbs

Manner Adverbs	Negation Adverbs	Time Adverbs
(adjective)+mente alto bajo bien mal mejor peor **Frequency Adverbs** a veces frecuentemente nunca raramente siempre **Place Adverbs** abajo acá adentro afuera alguna parte allá allí aquí arriba cerca delante detrás donde encima enfrente fuera todas partes	jamás ni no nunca tampoco **Inclusión Adverbs** además aún también **Quantity Adverbs** apenas bastante casi demasiado más menos mucho muy poco tanto **Interrogation Adverbs** ¿adónde? ¿cómo? ¿cuándo? ¿cuánto? ¿dónde? ¿por qué?	actualmente ahora anteayer ayer cuando después entonces hoy luego mañana mientras por fin pronto tarde temprano todavía ya **Point of View Adverbs** personalmente quizás evidentemente

Structure and Usage of Prepositions in Spanish

The preposition "**por**" is used to express the following:

- exchange, price, terms, units of measure, rate or multiplication
- to indicate a length of time (used only in America)
- the cause, motive, or reason for an action
- the means, manner, medium or instrument by which something is done
- indefinite or vague location
- on account of, for the sale of, on behalf of

The preposition "**para**" is used to express the following:

- destination
- purpose or use
- comparisons or contrasts
- a definite point in future time
- after "estar" to state something is about to happen

The preposition "**en**" is used to express the following:

- location
- proportion
- amount of time or money
- means
- compound prepositions
- functional neuter expressions

The preposition "**a**" is used to express the following:

- to indicate motion
- to connect a verb with a following infinitive
- to indicate manner or method
- to introduce a direct object that is a definite person or treated as a person
- to introduce an indirect object
- in various expressions of time
- preceding the pronouns (alguien, nadie, quien) when used as the direct object.

Structure and Usage of Personal Pronouns in Spanish

Subject Pronouns:

	Singular		**Plural**
I:	yo	**We**:	nosotros (m.), nosotras (fem.)
You:	tú, usted, vos	**You**:	vosotros (m.), vosotras (fem.), ustedes
He:	él	**They**:	ellos (m.), ellas (fem.)
She:	ella		

Subject pronouns are used for emphasizing or for clarifying the object.

The English pronoun "it" has no Spanish equivalent.

Reflexive Pronouns:

The reflexive pronoun is another form of an object pronoun, either direct or indirect. It indicates that the subject and the object of the verb are the same person or thing.

Reflexive pronouns (me, te, se, nos, os, se) generally precede the verb in simple and compound tenses or they may be tacked onto the end of verbs which are in the infinitive, gerund, or command forms.

Object pronouns (le, lo, la, los, les, las) are attached to affirmative commands.

With affirmative commands introduced by "que," the object pronoun always precedes the verb.

Certain verbs are often used with indirect object pronouns. They are "gustar," "agradar," "bastar," "doler," "faltar," "hacer," "faltar," "parecer," "quedar," "sobrar," and "tocar."

When a verb has two object pronouns, the indirect object pronoun precedes the direct object pronoun.

   -Le and –les change to "se" before lo, la, los, and las are added.

The preposition "a" is used before the direct object of a verb if the direct object is:

- a definite person or persons
- a domestic animal
- a geographic name
- a pronoun referring to a person

Demonstrative, Relative, and Possessive Pronouns in Spanish

Demonstrative Pronouns

This:	éste, ésta, esto
That:	ése, ésa, eso, aquél, aquélla, aquello
These:	éstos, éstas
Those:	ésos, ésas, aquéllos, aquéllas

Note: "esto," "eso" and "aquello" never take an accent.

Examples:

- Si éste hubiera jugado en nuestro equipo, habríamos ganado.

- No quiero eso.

- Ésa es mi favorita.

Relative Pronouns

Relative pronouns are used to introduce the clause of a sentence that describes the noun throughout the rest of the sentence.

que	that, who, which
el cual, la cual	the one who, the one which
los cuales, las cuales	those who, those which
el que, la que	the one who, the one which
los que , las que	those who, those which
lo que	that which, what, whatever
preposición + quien(es)	preposition + whom
preposición + que	preposition + that/which
cuyo, cuya, cuyos, cuyas	whose

Examples:

- El niño que está tocando la flauta es mi hermano.

- Para este juego puedes escoger a quienes quieras.

- El que crea que lo sabe, que levante la mano.

- Quienes quieran apuntarse a la excursión, que vengan mañana.

- Ese hombre, cuyas hijas son todas rubias, es vecino nuestro.

Possessive Adjectives

mi, mis	my
tu, tus	your
su, sus	his / her / your / its
nuestro-a, nuestros-as	our
vuestro-a, vuestros-as	your
su, sus	their

Examples:

- Mi casa es muy pequeña.

- Su camisa está todavía en la lavadora.

- Nuestras llaves han desaparecido.

- Da gusto ver vuestros vestidos recién planchados.

Possessive Pronouns

mío-a, míos-as	mine
tuyo-a, tuyos-as	yours
suyo-a, suyos-as	his / hers / yours / its
nuestro-a, nuestros-as	ours
vuestro-a, vuestros-as	yours
suyo-a, suyos-as	theirs

Examples:

- Cojamos tu coche, el mío está todavía en el taller de reparación.

- ¿Dónde están vuestros permisos de conducir? Los suyos los guardan siempre en la guantera del coche.

- Me parece que este dinero es suyo, Sra. Pérez.

- Si me caigo, la culpa será tuya.

Conjunctions and Contractions in Spanish

Conjunctions

y, e   and

o, u   or

ni   nor

pero   but

Examples:

- Él y yo nos fuimos a correr.
- Quieres que vaya o no.
- Me salió bien, pero fue por pura casualidad.
- No lo hice ni por ti ni por mí; lo hice por simple ética profesional.

Contractions

"al" = the contraction of the prepositions "a" and "el."

"del" = the contraction of the prepositions "de" and "el."

Examples:

- Nos vamos al campo
- Al bebé le gusta el biberón.
- Dice un refrán que del dicho al hecho, hay mucho trecho.
- Acabo de recortar este artículo del periódico de hoy.

VOCABULARY AND USAGE

Spanish language vocabulary changes at times according to the country where it is spoken. This is due to geographical and cultural influences. The lexicon below provides some examples of how vocabulary varies by country:

	ESPAÑA	COLOMBIA	MÉXICO	CHILE	ARGENTINA
PERSONAS	niño/joven	chino	chamaco	cabro	Pibe
	excelente	bacano	cool	súper	Macanudo
	cotilla	chismoso	farandulero		Cholulo
	bajo	bajito	chaparro		Petiso
	rubia	mona	rubia	rucia	Güera
	tonto	huevón/marica	güey	hueón	Boludo
	estadounidense	gringo	gringo estadounidense vecino del norte		Yankee

	ESPAÑA	COLOMBIA	MÉXICO	CHILE	ARGENTINA
COSAS	autobús	bus	camión	micro	Colectivo
	coche	carro	coche	auto	Auto
	cubo de la basura	caneca	basurero	cesto	Tacho
	bolígrafo	esfero	pluma	lápiz pasta	Birome
	lápiz	lapicero	lapicero		Portaminas
	pajilla	pitillo	popote	sorbete/cañita	sorbete/pajita
	ordenador	computadora	computadora	computadora	computadora
	teléfono móvil	celular	celular	celular	Celular
	vajilla	loza	trastes		Vajilla

	ESPAÑA	COLOMBIA	MÉXICO	CHILE	ARGENTINA
ROPA	chaqueta	chaqueta	chamarra	parka	Campera
	camiseta	camiseta	playera	polera	Remera
	zapatillas deportivas	tenis	tennis	zapatillas	Zapatillas

	ESPAÑA	COLOMBIA	MÉXICO	CHILE	ARGENTINA
COMIDA		arequipe	gajeta	manjar	dulce de leche
	judía	frijoles	frijóles	porotos	Porotos
	judía verde	habichuela	ejotes	porotos verdes	Chaucha
	refresco	gasimba	chesco	bebida	Refresco
	palomitas	maíz pira	palomitas	cabritas	pochocho

ACCIONES / ADJETIVOS	prisa	afán	apuro		Prisa
	estupendo	chévere	padre		Groso
	trabajo	trabajo	chamba	pega	Laburo
	estacionar/aparcar	parquear	aparcar/parquear	parquear	Estacionar
	soportar	aguantar	tragar		Bancar
	pereza	pereza	hueva		Fiaca
	conducir	manejar	manejar	manejar	Manejar
	coger	coger	agarrar	coger	Agarrar
LUGARES	piscina	piscina	alberca	piscina	Pileta
	discoteca	discoteca	antro	disco	Boliche
	fiesta	fiesta	pachanga	carrete	Juerga

Numbers and Dates in Spanish

When a noun's quantity is only one, use "un –a" for either masculine or feminine forms.

"Cien" is one hundred. When combined with other numbers of lesser quantities it becomes "ciento" or "cientos" in plural form (e.g., ciento dos, ocho cientos, cuatro cientos cincuenta y ocho). "Y" is not used to connect with other quantities. "Mil" is one thousand and stays so no matter how it is combined.

Numbers greater than 999 are written with a period for every greater set of numbers, not a comma. "Millón" is one million. For written quantities that do not include values in any places lesser than the millions value, a "de" is attached to the noun (e.g., cuatro millones de gatos, not cuatro millones tres gatos). There are no written designations for quantities larger than millions. A billion would be written: "mil millones." A trillion would be written" "mil millones de millones."

The days of the week, months, and seasons are not capitalized in Spanish. Dates are written day, month, year. When writing out the first day of the month, use "el primer día" or "el primero," otherwise, use cardinal numbers (e.g., domingo, quince de marzo; martes, catorce de enero…)

Idiomatic Usage in Spanish

Some of the moat common idiomatic expressions are:

- Andar/Estar en la luna – to be "out of it."
- Tomarse algo a la ligera – not taking serious what should be taken seriously
- Ir al grano – to go right to the heart of the matter
- Estar mal de la cabeza – to make illogical decisions
- Echar chispas – to be very angry
- Ir de mal en peor – to go from bad to worse
- Romperse la cabeza – to try to solve a very difficult problem
- Buscar cinco pies al gato – to complicate things
- Meter la pata – to put one's foot in it
- Rascarse el bolsillo – to be a generous financial donor
- Poner las manos en el fuego – to go right to the heart of the issue
- Andarse por las ramas – to ramble, not getting to the point

Proverbs and Sayings

The Spanish language is also very rich in "proverbs" or sayings:

- A mucha hambre, no hay pan duro.
  Beggars can't be choosers or for a good appetite there is no hard bread.

- A cada puerco le llega su San Martín.
  Everyone gets his comeuppance in the end / just desserts sooner or later.

- A donde el corazón se inclina, el pie camina.
  Home is where the heart is.

- A la ocasión la pintan calva.
  You have to make the most of the chances that come your way.

- A palabras necias, oídos sordos.
  Take no notice of the stupid things people say.

- A pan de quince días, hambre de tres semanas.
  Beggars can't be choosers, for a good appetite there is no hard bread, or when one is hungry everything tastes good.

- A rey muerto, rey puesto.
  As soon as one goes out the window, another comes in the door.

- Algo es algo; menos es nada.
    Half a loaf is better than no bread.

- Borrón y cuenta nueva.
    Let bygones be bygones.

- Cada uno habla de la feria según le va en ella.
    Everyone sees things from his / her own point of view.

- Como quien oye llover.
    It's like water off a duck's back.

- Allí donde fueres, haz lo que vieres.
    When in Rome, do as the Romans do.

Negative and Interrogative Constructions in Spanish

Negative Constructions

The word "no" is placed before a verb to make a negative meaning. "No" is repeated to affirm the negative construction to a yes or no question.

Examples:

-¿Quieres correr?
-No, no me gusta correr.

Interrogative Constructions

Qué	inquires about actions
Cuál, Cuáles	inquires about statements
Quién, Quiénes	inquires about person(s)
Cuánto, Cuánta, Cuántos, Cuántas	inquires about quantity
Cómo	inquires about occurrence

Structure and usage of Commands in Spanish

As in English, commands are used when we tell someone what to do.

How to form commands:

- The polite commands (singular and plural) take the same form as the present subjunctive.
- The singular of the familiar command is the same as the third person singular of the present indicative.
- Object pronouns are added to all affirmative commands.
- All negative commands take the same form as the corresponding person in the present subjunctive.
- In negative commands, the object pronouns precede the verb.
- Indirect commands are always expressed by the present subjunctive and are usually introduced by "que."

The only irregular commands occur in the affirmative singular (tú) and are as follows:

- Decir – di
- Hacer – haz
- Ir – ve
- Poner – pon
- Salir – sal
- Ser – sé
- Tener – ten
- Venir – ven

Structure and Usage of Comparative Constructions

Mi perro caza tan bien como el tuyo.
Comparative Equality

Mi casa es tan grande como la de mi hermano.
Comparative Equality

Esta moneda vale menos que un dólar.
Comparative Inequality

Eres más alto que mi primo.
Comparative Inequality

Esa playa es la más bonita de Colombia.
Absolute Superlative

Ese plato es el menos pedido del menú.

Absolute Superlative

III. INTERPRETIVE READING

Using Interpretive Reading Skills for Understanding Written Materials

El coronel volvió a abrirse paso, sin mirar a nadie, aturdido por los aplausos y los gritos, y salió a la calle con el gallo bajo el brazo.

Todo el pueblo –la gente de abajo– salió a verlo pasar seguido por los niños de la escuela. Un negro gigantesco trepado en una mesa y con una culebra enrollada en el cuello vendía medicinas sin licencia en una esquina de la plaza. De regreso del puerto un grupo numeroso se había detenido a escuchar su pregón. Pero cuando pasó el coronel con el gallo la atención se desplazó hacia él. Nunca había sido tan largo el camino de su casa.

No se arrepintió. Desde hacía mucho tiempo el pueblo yacía en una especie de sopor, estragado por diez años de historia. Esa tarde –otro viernes sin carta– la gente había despertado. El coronel se acordó de otra época. Se vio a sí mismo con su mujer y su hijo asistiendo bajo el paraguas a un espectáculo que no fue interrumpido a pesar de la lluvia. Se acordó de los dirigentes de su partido, escrupulosamente peinados, abanicándose en el patio de su casa al compás de la música. Revivió casi la dolorosa resonancia del bombo en sus intestinos.

Cruzó por la calle paralela al río, y también allí encontró la tumultuosa muchedumbre de los remotos domingos electorales. Observaban el descargue del circo. Desde el interior de una tienda una mujer gritó algo relacionado con el gallo. Él siguió absorto hasta su casa, todavía oyendo voces dispersas, como si lo persiguieran los desperdicios de la ovación de la gallera.

En la puerta se dirigió a los niños.

—Todos para su casa —dijo—. Al que entre, lo saco a correazos.

Puso la tranca y se dirigió directamente a la cocina. Su mujer salió asfixiándose del dormitorio.

—Se lo llevaron a la fuerza —gritó—. Les dije que el gallo no saldría de esta casa mientras yo estuviera viva.

El coronel amarró el gallo al soporte de la hornilla. Cambió el agua al tarro, perseguido por la voz frenética de la mujer.

—Dijeron que se lo llevarían por encima de nuestros cadáveres —dijo—. Dijeron que el gallo no era nuestro, sino de todo el pueblo.

Sólo cuando terminó con el gallo, el coronel se enfrentó al rostro trastornado de su mujer. Descubrió sin asombro que no le producía remordimiento ni compasión.

—Hicieron bien —dijo calmadamente. Y luego, registrándose los bolsillos, agregó, con una especie de insondable dulzura—: El gallo no se vende.

Ella lo siguió hasta el dormitorio. Lo sintió completamente humano, pero inasible, como si lo estuviera viendo en la pantalla de un cine. El coronel extrajo del ropero un rollo de billetes, lo juntó al que tenía en lo bolsillos, contó el total y lo guardó en el ropero.

—Ahí hay veintinueve pesos para devolvérselos a mi compadre Sabas —dijo—. El resto se le paga cuando venga la pensión.

—Y si no viene... —preguntó la mujer.

—Vendrá.

—Pero si no viene...

—Pues entonces no se le paga.

Encontró los zapatos nuevos debajo de la cama. Volvió al armario por la caja de cartón, limpió la suela con un trapo y metió los zapatos en la caja, como los llevó su esposa el domingo en la noche. Ella no se movió.

—Los zapatos se devuelven —dijo el coronel—. Son trece pesos más para mi compadre.

—No los reciben —dijo ella.

—Tienen que recibirlos —replicó el coronel—. Sólo me los he puesto dos veces.

—Los turcos no entienden de esas cosas —dijo la mujer.

—Tienen que entender.

—Y si no entienden...
—Pues entonces que no entiendan.

Se acostaron sin comer. El coronel esperó a que su mujer terminara el rosario para apagar la lámpara. Pero no pudo dormir. Oyó las campanas de la censura cinematográfica, y casi en seguida –tres horas después– el toque de queda. La pedregosa respiración de la mujer se hizo angustiosa con el aire helado de la madrugada. El coronel tenía aún los ojos abiertos cuando ella habló con una voz reposada, conciliatoria.
—Estás despierto.
—Sí.
—Trata de entrar en razón –dijo la mujer–. Habla mañana con mi compadre Sabas.
—No viene hasta el lunes.
—Mejor –dijo la mujer–. Así tendrás tres días para recapacitar.
—No hay nada que recapacitar –dijo el coronel.

El viscoso aire de octubre había sido sustituido por una frescura apacible. El coronel volvió a reconocer a diciembre en el horario de los alcaravanes. Cuando dieron las dos, todavía no había podido dormir. Pero sabía que su mujer también estaba despierta. Trató de cambiar de posición en la hamaca.

—Estás desvelado –dijo la mujer.
—Sí.
Ella pensó un momento.
—No estamos en condiciones de hacer esto –dijo–. Ponte a pensar cuántos son cuatrocientos pesos juntos.
—Ya falta poco para que venga la pensión –dijo el coronel–.
—Estás diciendo lo mismo desde hace quince años.
—Por eso –dijo el coronel–. Ya no puede demorar mucho más.
Ella hizo un silencio. Pero cuando volvió a hablar, al coronel le pareció que el tiempo no había transcurrido.
—Tengo la impresión de que esa plata no llegará nunca –dijo la mujer.
—Llegará.
—Y si no llega...

Él no encontró la voz para responder. Al primer canto del gallo tropezó con la realidad, pero volvió a hundirse en un sueño denso, seguro, sin remordimientos. Cuando despertó, ya el sol estaba alto. Su mujer dormía. El coronel repitió metódicamente, con dos horas de retraso, sus movimientos matinales, y esperó a su esposa para desayunar.

Ella se levantó impenetrable. Se dieron los buenos días y se sentaron a desayunar en silencio. El coronel sorbió una taza de café negro acompañada con un pedazo de queso y un pan de dulce. Pasó toda la mañana en la sastrería. A la una volvió a la casa y encontró a su mujer remendando entre las begonias.
—Es hora del almuerzo —dijo.
—No hay almuerzo —dijo la mujer.

Él se encogió de hombros. Trató de tapar los portillos de la cerca del patio para evitar que los niños entraran a la cocina. Cuando regresó al corredor, la mesa estaba servida.

En el curso del almuerzo el coronel comprendió que su esposa se estaba forzando para no llorar. Esa certidumbre lo alarmó. Conocía el carácter de su mujer, naturalmente duro, y endurecido todavía más por cuarenta años de amargura. La muerte de su hijo no le arrancó una lágrima.

Fijó directamente en sus ojos una mirada de reprobación. Ella se mordió los labios, se secó los párpados con la manga y siguió almorzando.

—Eres un desconsiderado —dijo.
El coronel no habló.
—Eres caprichoso, terco y desconsiderado —repitió ella. Cruzó los cubiertos sobre el plato, pero en seguida rectificó supersticiosamente la posición—. Toda una vida comiendo tierra, para que ahora resulte que merezco menos consideración que un gallo.
—Es distinto —dijo el coronel.
—Es lo mismo —replicó la mujer—. Debías darte cuenta de que me estoy muriendo, que esto que tengo no es una enfermedad, sino una agonía.

El coronel no habló hasta cuando no terminó de almorzar.

—Si el doctor me garantiza que vendiendo el gallo se te quita el asma, lo vendo en seguida —dijo—. Pero si no, no.

Esa tarde llevó el gallo a la gallera. De regreso encontró a su esposa al borde de la crisis. Se paseaba a lo largo del corredor, el cabello suelto a la espalda, los brazos abiertos, buscando el aire por encima del silbido de sus pulmones. Allí estuvo hasta la prima noche. Luego se acostó sin dirigirse a su marido.

Masticó oraciones hasta un poco después del toque de queda. Entonces el coronel se dispuso a apagar la lámpara. Pero ella se opuso.

—No quiero morirme en tinieblas —dijo.

El coronel dejó la lámpara en el suelo. Empezaba a sentirse agotado. Tenía deseos de olvidarse de todo, de dormir de un tirón cuarenta y cuatro días y despertar el veinte de enero a las tres de la tarde, en la gallera y en el momento exacto de soltar el gallo, pero se sabía amenazado por la vigilia de la mujer.

—Es la misma historia de siempre —comenzó ella un momento después—. Nosotros ponemos el hambre para que coman los otros. Es la misma historia desde hace cuarenta años.

El coronel guardó silencio hasta cuando su esposa hizo una pausa para preguntarle si estaba despierto. Él respondió que sí. La mujer continuó en un tono liso, fluyente, implacable.

—Todo el mundo ganará con el gallo, menos nosotros. Somos los únicos que no tenemos ni un centavo para apostar.

—El dueño del gallo tiene derecho a un veinte por ciento.

—También tenías derecho a tu pensión de veterano después de exponer el pellejo en la guerra civil. Ahora todo el mundo tiene su vida asegurada, y tú estás muerto de hambre, completamente solo.

—No estoy solo —dijo el coronel.

Trató de explicar algo, pero lo venció el sueño. Ella siguió hablando sordamente hasta cuando se dio cuenta de que su esposo dormía. Entonces salió del mosquitero y se paseó por la sala en tinieblas. Allí siguió hablando. El coronel la llamó en la madrugada.

Ella apareció en la puerta, espectral, iluminada desde abajo por la lámpara casi extinguida. La apagó antes de entrar al mosquitero. Pero siguió hablando.
—Vamos a hacer una cosa —la interrumpió el coronel.
—Lo único que se puede hacer es vender el gallo —dijo la mujer.
—También se puede vender el reloj.
—No lo compran.
—Mañana trataré de que Álvaro me dé los cuarenta pesos.
—No te los da.
—Entonces se vende el cuadro.

Cuando la mujer volvió a hablar estaba otra vez fuera del mosquitero. El coronel percibió su respiración impregnada de hierbas medicinales.

—No lo compran —dijo.
—Ya veremos —dijo el coronel suavemente, sin un rastro de alteración en la voz—. Ahora duérmete. Si mañana no se puede vender nada, se pensará en otra cosa.

Trató de tener los ojos abiertos, pero lo quebrantó el sueño. Cayó hasta el fondo de una substancia sin tiempo y sin espacio, donde las palabras de su mujer tenían un significado diferente. Pero un instante después se sintió sacudido por el hombro.

—Contéstame.

El coronel no supo si había oído esa palabra antes o después del sueño. Estaba amaneciendo. La ventana se recortaba en la claridad verde del domingo. Pensó que tenía fiebre. Le ardían los ojos y tuvo que hacer un gran esfuerzo para recobrar la lucidez.

–Qué se puede hacer si no se puede vender nada – repitió la mujer.
–Entonces ya será veinte de enero –dijo el coronel, perfectamente consciente–. El veinte por ciento lo pagan esa misma tarde.
–Si el gallo gana –dijo la mujer–. Pero si pierde. No se te ha ocurrido que el gallo puede perder.
–Es un gallo que no puede perder.
–Pero suponte que pierda.
–Todavía faltan cuarenta y cinco días para empezar a pensar en eso –dijo el coronel.
La mujer se desesperó.
–Y mientras tanto ¿qué comemos?, –preguntó, y agarró al coronel por el cuello de la franela. Lo sacudió con energía.
–Dime, qué comemos.

El coronel necesitó setenta y cinco años –los setenta y cinco años de su vida, minuto a minuto– para llegar a ese instante. Se sintió puro, explícito, invencible, en el momento de responder:
–Los Demonios.

El coronel no tiene quien le escriba, by Gabriel García Márquez, 1958. *In Google book search, Google.* Retrieved April 10, 2006 from:
http://books.google.com/books?ie=UTF-8&id=n7V6eF32nOoC&dq=Gabriel+garc%C3%ADa+m%C3%A1rquez+%2Bcoronel&psp=wp&pg=PR4&printsec=3&lpg=PR4&sig=Wp6uzGbQxpwligSRsfATHnypjFo

Answer the following questions about the above written example

1. In the last sentence, on the fourth page in the passage, what does the colonel's wife mean?

    A. She doesn't want to die suffering.

    B. She wants the lights turned on.

    C. She says that with the lights turned off she will die.

    D. She doesn't want to die in the fog.

    Answer: B

2. What feeling is expressed by the colonel, in the passage's closing words, spoken to his wife?

    A. Hate

    B. Love

    C. Abandonment

    D. Envy

    Answer: C

TEACHER CERTIFICATION STUDY GUIDE

Now, read this sample and answer the following questions.

Claudio: Hola. ¿Cómo has estado?

Don Fintesco: Perfecto. ¿Qué necesitas?

Claudio: Pues te cuento, tengo mucha plata. Mis negocios van bien. Ahora te voy a proponer una nueva empresa en la cual tú me puedes ayudar. Resulta que en mis viajes conocí una princesa sueca y ella me habló de su amor por las esmeraldas y la falta de aquéllas en su colección personal. Naturalmente le ofrecí mi ayuda.

Don Fintesco: Se pone interesante tu cuento. ¿Cuánto crees que va ella a pagar por la piedra de sus sueños?

Claudio: No es para soñar, sino para vivir, mi apreciado amigo. Ella llega este viernes y tu tarea es de darme a mí no antes del jueves en la media noche, una piedra de quince quilates.

Don Fintesco: ¿Cómo que estás loco? ¿Dónde voy a encontrar una piedra así en tres días? ¿Adentro de mi zapato?

Claudio: No me importan los detalles, tráela el jueves y te daré cuarenta por ciento de lo que gane en la venta. ¡Hasta entonces, amigo!

1. **The third time Don Fintesco speaks he uses "Cómo" as an adverb. How does that change the quality of what he is expressing?**

    A. He is showing surprise and incredulous disbelief at Claudio's request.

    B. He is addressing Claudio because he is insane.

    C. He is asking Claudio why he is losing his sanity.

    D. He is disrespecting Claudio.

    Answer: A

Daily-life, Specialized, and Reference Materials

Reading 1

¿Me puedes hacer el favor de explicar, amigo mío, qué hace un hombre al despertarse y cómo se viste cuando va a salir para trabajar? Primero se baña; después se pone la ropa interior; la camisa con cuello y la corbata; los calcetines; el pantalón y un par de zapatos; el chaleco y el saco. Toma el desayuno y, antes de salir para la calle, se pone el sombrero y la chaqueta.

1. **What does a man do when he wakes up and before he goes out to work?**

    a. He washes himself.

    b. He washes himself, gets dressed, and has breakfast.

    c. He gets dressed, has breakfast, and wears his hat and jacket.

    d. He gets dressed and, before he goes out, he puts on his hat and jacket.

    Answer: B

Reading 2

Nos gustaba la casa porque aparte de espaciosa y antigua (hoy que las casas antiguas sucumben a la más ventajosa liquidación de sus materiales) guardaba los recuerdos de nuestros bisabuelos, el abuelo paterno, nuestros padres y toda la infancia. Nos habituamos Irene y yo a persistir solos en ella, lo que era una locura pues en esa casa podían vivir ocho personas sin estorbarse. Hacíamos la limpieza por la mañana, levantándonos a las siete, y a eso de las once yo le dejaba a Irene las últimas habitaciones por repasar y me iba a la cocina. Almorzábamos al mediodía, siempre puntuales; ya no quedaba nada por hacer fuera de unos platos sucios. Nos resultaba grato almorzar pensando en la casa profunda y silenciosa y cómo nos bastábamos para mantenerla limpia. A veces llegábamos a creer que era ella la que no nos dejó casarnos. Irene rechazó dos pretendientes sin mayor motivo, a mí se me murió María Esther antes que llegáramos a comprometernos.

Entramos en los cuarenta años con la inexpresada idea de que el nuestro, simple y silencioso matrimonio de hermanos, era necesaria clausura de la genealogía asentada por nuestros bisabuelos en nuestra casa. Nos moriríamos allí algún día, vagos y esquivos primos se quedarían con la casa y la echarían al suelo para enriquecerse con el terreno y los ladrillos; o mejor, nosotros mismos la voltearíamos justicieramente antes de que fuese demasiado tarde.

Irene era una chica nacida para no molestar a nadie. Aparte de su actividad matinal se pasaba el resto del día tejiendo en el sofá de su dormitorio. No sé por qué tejía tanto, yo creo que las mujeres tejen cuando han encontrado en esa labor el gran pretexto para no hacer nada. Irene no era así, tejía cosas siempre necesarias, tricotas para el invierno, medias para mí, mañanitas y chalecos para ella. A veces tejía un chaleco y después lo destejía en un momento porque algo no le agradaba; era gracioso ver en la canastilla el montón de lana encrespada resistiéndose a perder su forma de algunas horas. Los sábados iba yo al centro a comprarle lana; Irene tenía fe en mi gusto, se complacía con los colores y nunca tuve que devolver madejas.

Yo aprovechaba esas salidas para dar una vuelta por las librerías y preguntar vanamente si había novedades en literatura francesa. Desde 1939 no llegaba nada valioso a la Argentina. Pero es de la casa que me interesa hablar, de la casa y de Irene, porque yo no tengo importancia.

Me pregunto qué hubiera hecho Irene sin el tejido. Uno puede releer un libro, pero cuando un pullover está terminado no se puede repetirlo sin escándalo. Un día encontré el cajón de abajo de la cómoda de alcanfor lleno de pañoletas blancas, verdes, lilas. Estaban con naftalina, apiladas como en una mercería; no tuve valor para preguntarle a Irene qué pensaba hacer con ellas. No necesitábamos ganarnos la vida, todos los meses llegaba plata de los campos y el dinero aumentaba. Pero a Irene solamente la entretenía el tejido, mostraba una destreza maravillosa y a mí se me iban las horas viéndole las manos como erizos plateados, agujas yendo y viniendo y una o dos canastillas en el suelo donde se agitaban constantemente los ovillos. Era hermoso.

Cómo no acordarme de la distribución de la casa. El comedor, una sala con gobelinos, la biblioteca y tres dormitorios grandes quedaban en la parte mas retirada, la que mira hacia Rodríguez Peña. Solamente un pasillo con su maciza puerta de roble aislaba esa parte del ala delantera donde había un baño, la cocina, nuestros dormitorios y el *living* central, al cual comunicaban los dormitorios y el pasillo. Se entraba a la casa por un zaguán con mayólica, y la puerta cancel daba al *living*. De manera que uno entraba por el zaguán, abría la cancel y pasaba al *living*; tenía a los lados las puertas de nuestros dormitorios, y al frente el pasillo que conducía a la parte mas retirada; avanzando por el pasillo se franqueaba la puerta de roble y mas allá empezaba el otro lado de la casa, o bien se podía girar a la izquierda justamente antes de la puerta y seguir por un pasillo más estrecho que llevaba a la cocina y al baño. Cuando la puerta estaba abierta advertía uno que la casa era muy grande; si no, daba la impresión de un departamento de los que se edifican ahora, apenas para moverse; Irene y yo vivíamos siempre en esta parte de la casa, casi nunca íbamos más allá de la puerta de roble, salvo para hacer la limpieza, pues es increíble cómo se junta tierra en los muebles. Buenos Aires será una ciudad limpia, pero eso lo debe a sus habitantes y no a otra cosa.

Hay demasiada tierra en el aire, apenas sopla una ráfaga se palpa el polvo en los mármoles de las consolas y entre los rombos de las carpetas de macramé; da trabajo sacarlo bien con plumero, vuela y se suspende en el aire, un momento después se deposita de nuevo en los muebles y los pianos.

Lo recordaré siempre con claridad porque fue simple y sin circunstancias inútiles. Irene estaba tejiendo en su dormitorio, eran las ocho de la noche y de repente se me ocurrió poner al fuego la pavita del mate. Fui por el pasillo hasta enfrentar la entornada puerta de roble, y daba la vuelta al codo que llevaba a la cocina cuando escuché algo en el comedor o en la biblioteca. El sonido venía impreciso y sordo, como un volcarse de silla sobre la alfombra o un ahogado susurro de conversación. También lo oí, al mismo tiempo o un segundo después, en el fondo del pasillo que traía desde aquellas piezas hasta la puerta. Me tiré contra la pared antes de que fuera demasiado tarde, la cerré de golpe apoyando el cuerpo; felizmente la llave estaba puesta de nuestro lado y además corrí el gran cerrojo para más seguridad.

Fui a la cocina, calenté la pavita, y cuando estuve de vuelta con la bandeja del mate le dije a Irene:

—Tuve que cerrar la puerta del pasillo. Han tomado parte del fondo.
Dejó caer el tejido y me miró con sus graves ojos cansados.
—¿Estás seguro?
Asentí.
—Entonces —dijo recogiendo las agujas— tendremos que vivir en este lado.

Yo cebaba el mate con mucho cuidado, pero ella tardó un rato en reanudar su labor. Me acuerdo que me tejía un chaleco gris; a mí me gustaba ese chaleco.

Los primeros días nos pareció penoso porque ambos habíamos dejado en la parte tomada muchas cosas que queríamos. Mis libros de literatura francesa, por ejemplo, estaban todos en la biblioteca. Irene pensó en una botella de Hesperidina de muchos años. Con frecuencia (pero esto solamente sucedió los primeros días), cerrábamos algún cajón de las cómodas y nos mirábamos con tristeza.

–No está aquí.

Y era una cosa más de todo lo que habíamos perdido al otro lado de la casa.

Pero también tuvimos ventajas. La limpieza se simplificó tanto que aun levantándose tardísimo, a las nueve y media por ejemplo, no daban las once y ya estábamos de brazos cruzados. Irene se acostumbró a ir conmigo a la cocina y ayudarme a preparar el almuerzo. Lo pensamos bien, y se decidió esto: mientras yo preparaba el almuerzo, Irene cocinaría platos para comer fríos de noche. Nos alegramos porque siempre resultaba molesto tener que abandonar los dormitorios al atardecer y ponerse a cocinar. Ahora nos bastaba con la mesa en el dormitorio de Irene y las fuentes de comida fiambre.

Irene estaba contenta porque le quedaba más tiempo para tejer. Yo andaba un poco perdido a causa de los libros, pero por no afligir a mi hermana me puse a revisar la colección de estampillas de papá, y eso me sirvió para matar el tiempo. Nos divertíamos mucho, cada uno en sus cosas, casi siempre reunidos en el dormitorio de Irene que era más cómodo. A veces Irene decía:

–Fíjate en este punto que se me ha ocurrido. ¿No da un dibujo de trébol?

Un rato después, era yo el que le ponía ante los ojos un cuadradito de papel para que viese el mérito de algún sello de Eupen y Malmédy. Estábamos bien, y poco a poco empezábamos a no pensar. Se puede vivir sin pensar.

Cuando Irene soñaba en alta voz yo me desvelaba en seguida. Nunca pude habituarme a esa voz de estatua o papagayo, voz que viene de los sueños y no de la garganta. Irene decía que mis sueños consistían en grandes sacudones que a veces hacían caer el cobertor. Nuestros dormitorios tenían el *living* de por medio, pero de noche se escuchaba cualquier cosa en la casa. Nos oíamos respirar, toser, presentíamos el ademán que conduce a la llave del velador, los mutuos y frecuentes insomnios.

(Aparte de eso, todo estaba callado en la casa. De día eran los rumores domésticos, el roce metálico de las agujas de tejer, un crujido al pasar las hojas del álbum filatélico. La puerta de roble, creo haberlo dicho, era maciza. En la cocina y el baño, que quedaban tocando la parte tomada, nos poníamos a hablar en voz más alta o Irene cantaba canciones de cuna. En una cocina hay demasiados ruidos de loza y vidrios para que otros sonidos irrumpan en ella. Muy pocas veces permitíamos allí el silencio, pero cuando tornábamos a los dormitorios y al *living*, entonces la casa se ponía callada y a media luz, hasta pisábamos despacio para no molestarnos. Yo creo que era por eso que de noche, cuando Irene empezaba a soñar en alta voz, me desvelaba en seguida.)

Es casi repetir lo mismo salvo las consecuencias. De noche siento sed, y antes de acostarnos le dije a Irene que iba hasta la cocina a servirme un vaso de agua. Desde la puerta del dormitorio (ella tejía), oí ruido en la cocina; tal vez en la cocina o tal vez en el baño porque el codo del pasillo apagaba el sonido. A Irene le llamo la atención mi brusca manera de detenerme, y vino a mi lado sin decir palabra. Nos quedamos escuchando los ruidos, notando claramente que eran de este lado de la puerta de roble, en la cocina y el baño, o en el pasillo mismo donde empezaba el codo casi al lado nuestro.

No nos miramos siquiera. Apreté el brazo de Irene y la hice correr conmigo hasta la puerta cancel, sin volvernos hacia atrás. Los ruidos se oían mas fuerte pero siempre sordos, a espaldas nuestras. Cerré de un golpe la cancel y nos quedamos en el zaguán. Ahora no se oía nada.

—Han tomado esta parte —dijo Irene. El tejido le colgaba de las manos y las hebras iban hasta la cancel y se perdían debajo. Cuando vio que los ovillos habían quedado del otro lado, soltó el tejido sin mirarlo.

—¿Tuviste tiempo de traer alguna cosa? —le pregunté inútilmente.
—No, nada.

Estábamos con lo puesto. Me acordé de los quince mil pesos en el armario de mi dormitorio. Ya era tarde ahora.

Como me quedaba el reloj pulsera, vi que eran las once de la noche. Rodeé con mi brazo la cintura de Irene (yo creo que ella estaba llorando) y salimos así a la calle. Antes de alejarnos tuve lástima, cerré bien la puerta de entrada y tiré la llave a la alcantarilla. No fuese que a algún pobre diablo se le ocurriera robar y se metiera en la casa, a esa hora y con la casa tomada.

Casa tomada, by Julio Cortázar, from *Bestiario*, 1951. Retrieved Nov 30, 2010 from:
http://www.lainsignia.org/2001/enero/cul_031.htm

1. **Why do the characters in this short story like their house, apart from it being big and spacious?**

    A. Because it is full of memories from their ancestors.

    B. Because eight people could live in it and not get in each other's way.

    C. Because they could profit from selling its construction materials.

    D. Because it is a quiet old house.

    Answer: A

2. **Which feeling(s) best reflect the setting in the story?**

    A. Sadness and abandonment

    B. Boredom

    C. Apathy

    D. Solitude and attachment

    Answer: D

3. **What do you think the strange sounds and movements that make the characters flee the house represent?**

   A. Their fears and dislikes.

   B. The activity of a supernatural being.

   C. Nothing.

   D. The sounds and movements of burglars.

   Answer: A

   * * *

Reading 3

Había empezado a leer la novela unos días antes. La abandonó por negocios urgentes, volvió a abrirla cuando regresaba en tren a la finca; se dejaba interesar lentamente por la trama, por el dibujo de los personajes.

Esa tarde, después de escribir una carta a su apoderado y discutir con el mayordomo una cuestión de aparcerías volvió al libro en la tranquilidad del estudio que miraba hacia el parque de los robles.

Arrellanado en su sillón favorito de espaldas a la puerta que lo hubiera molestado como una irritante posibilidad de intrusiones, dejó que su mano izquierda acariciara una y otra vez el terciopelo verde y se puso a leer los últimos capítulos. Su memoria retenía sin esfuerzo los nombres y las imágenes de los protagonistas; la ilusión novelesca lo ganó casi en seguida. Gozaba del placer casi perverso de irse desgajando línea a línea de lo que lo rodeaba, y sentir a la vez que su cabeza descansaba cómodamente en el terciopelo del alto respaldo, que los cigarrillos seguían al alcance de la mano, que más allá de los ventanales danzaba el aire del atardecer bajo los robles. Palabra a palabra, absorbido por la sórdida disyuntiva de los héroes, dejándose ir hacia las imágenes que se concertaban y adquirían color y movimiento, fue testigo del último encuentro en la cabaña del monte.

Primero entraba la mujer, recelosa; ahora llegaba el amante, lastimada la cara por el chicotazo de una rama. Admirablemente restallaba ella la sangre con sus besos, pero él rechazaba las caricias, no había venido para repetir las ceremonias de una pasión secreta, protegida por un mundo de hojas secas y senderos furtivos. El puñal se entibiaba contra su pecho, y debajo latía la libertad agazapada. Un diálogo anhelante corría por las páginas como un arroyo de serpientes, y se sentía que todo estaba decidido desde siempre. Hasta esas caricias que enredaban el cuerpo del amante como queriendo retenerlo y disuadirlo, dibujaban abominablemente la figura de otro cuerpo que era necesario destruir. Nada había sido olvidado: coartadas, azares, posibles errores. A partir de esa hora cada instante tenía su empleo minuciosamente atribuido. El doble repaso despiadado se interrumpía apenas para que una mano acariciara una mejilla.

Empezaba a anochecer.

Sin mirarse ya, atados rígidamente a la tarea que los esperaba, se separaron en la puerta de la cabaña. Ella debía seguir por la senda que iba al norte. Desde la senda opuesta él se volvió un instante para verla correr con el pelo suelto. Corrió a su vez, parapetándose en los árboles y los setos, hasta distinguir en la bruma malva del crepúsculo la alameda que llevaba a la casa. Los perros no debían ladrar, y no ladraron. El mayordomo no estaría a esa hora, y no estaba. Subió los tres peldaños del porche y entró.

Desde la sangre galopando en sus oídos le llegaban las palabras de la mujer: primero una sala azul, después una galería, una escalera alfombrada. En lo alto, dos puertas. Nadie en la primera habitación, nadie en la segunda. La puerta del salón, y entonces el puñal en la mano. La luz de los ventanales, el alto respaldo de un sillón de terciopelo verde, la cabeza del hombre en el sillón leyendo una novela.

Continuidad de los parques, by Julio Cortázar, from *Final del juego*. Retrieved December 2, 2010 from:
http://www.literatura.org/Cortazar/Continuidad.html

TEACHER CERTIFICATION STUDY GUIDE

1. What two stories converge in this short story?

    A. The story of the man reading the novel and the story of the women

    B. There is only one story.

    C. The story of the man reading the novel and the novel itself.

    D. There are three stories, not two.

    Answer: C

2. What is the story about?

    A. The man's own life.

    B. The story of another man's life.

    C. About business.

    D. The story of a hunted novel.

    Answer: A

3. To which literary genre belongs *Continuidad de los paques*?

    A. Horror

    B. Fantasy

    C. Romantic

    D. Science Fiction

    Answer: B

Reading 4

> Tirada en el campo estaba desde hacía tiempo una Flauta que ya nadie tocaba, hasta que un día un Burro que paseaba por ahí resopló fuerte sobre ella haciéndola producir el sonido más dulce de su vida, es decir, de la vida del Burro y de la Flauta.
>
> Incapaces de comprender lo que había pasado, pues la racionalidad no era su fuerte y ambos creían en la racionalidad, se separaron presurosos, avergonzados de lo mejor que el uno y el otro habían hecho durante su triste existencia.
>
> ***El burro y la flauta***, de *La oveja negra y demás fábulas,* by Augusto Monterroso. Retrieved December 4, 2010 from:
> http://www.ciudadseva.com/textos/cuentos/esp/monte/burro.htm

1. **Why do you think the author picked the donkey and the flute as main characters?**

    A. Because they are funny.

    B. Because they are dumb.

    C. Because fable characters are often animals and objects.

    D. Because they are, apparently, opposites.

    Answer: B

2. **What is the moral in this fable?**

    A. Animals and objects are not rational.

    B. Donkeys can play music.

    C. Flutes and donkeys are friends.

    D. Sometimes we are ashamed of great things we did without knowing how, because we are ignorant.

    Answer: D

IV. CULTURAL PERSPECTIVES

Development and Spread of the Spanish Language in Spain and Latin America

Most Spanish dialects have two second-person singular pronouns, one for informal use and one for more formal treatment. In most dialects the informal pronoun is "tú," which comes directly from Latin, and the formal pronoun is "usted," which is usually considered to originate from "vuestra merced," (Your grace) - though others have traced it to the Arabic "Ustad, professor/sir."

In a number of regions "tú" is replaced by another pronoun -"vos," and the verb conjugation changes accordingly. "Vos" comes from Latin "vos," which was simply the second person plural informal pronoun.

In Spain "tú" is informal -to friends and "usted" is formal -to elders. In parts of Spain fifty years ago, a child would not use "tú" but "usted," to address a parent. Chileans employ "usted" to address children to parents and also parents to children. In Cuba "tú" is used even in very formal circumstances and "usted" remains seldom used. In most of inland Colombia, "usted" is the pronoun of choice for all situations even when speaking between friends or family, but in the country's capital the use of "tú" is more accepted in informal situations, especially between young interlocutors of the opposite sex andamong young women. In the Caribbean coast "tú" is used for practically all informal situations and many formal situations, "usted" being reserved for the most formal environments.

Tuteo

It consists in using the second person singular pronoun "tú" informally, especially in contexts where "usted" is to be grammatically expected. The notion's corresponding verb is "tutear"- a transitive verb. *Tuteo* is used even in those dialects where the informal pronoun is "vos." It is prevalent in Chile, Cuba, and Colombia. It is used particularly to address family or friends and suggests an intimate tone to personal reference.

Voseo

It is the use of the second person singular pronoun "vos" in several Spanish dialects, instead of "tú," which is often considered standard. "Vos" is used extensively as the primary spoken form of the second-person singular in various countries around Latin America, including Argentina, Costa Rica, Ecuador, El Salvador, Guatemala, Honduras, the Zulia State, Venezuela, various regions of Colombia, Nicaragua, Paraguay and Uruguay. But only in Argentina, Uruguay, and increasingly in Paraguay, it is also the standard written form.

This phenomenon is also gradually taking place in Central America, where the most prestigious media outlets are beginning to use the pronoun "vos" instead of "tú."

Distinción

It refers to the differentiated pronunciation of the two Spanish phonemes written ‹s› and ‹z› or ‹c› (only before ‹e› or ‹i›, the so-called "soft" ‹c›):

This pronunciation is the standard on which Spanish orthography was based, and it is universal in Central and Northern parts of Spain. In Spanish the choice between the spellings ‹sa›, ‹se›, ‹si›, ‹so›, ‹su› and ‹za›, ‹ce›, ‹ci›, ‹zo›, ‹zu› is determined by the pronunciation in most of Spain, where it is often done according to etymology or orthographic conventions.

Ceceo

It is a linguistic phenomenon found in a few dialects of southern Spain in which the historical phonemes /s/ and /θ/ are both realized as [θ] ("th" sound). In other words, only the latter sound is used for ‹s›, ‹z›, and soft ‹c›.

Ceceo is found primarily in some varieties of Andalusian Spanish, and there is some evidence of it in parts of Central America.

Seseo

It is the phenomenon in the opposite direction: the original phonemes /s/ and /θ/ ("th" sound) are both pronounced as [s].

Seseo is found primarily in some varieties of Andalusian Spanish and all speakers in Hispanic America are seseantes, being the seseo consider standar in all varieties of Latin American Spanish. In Spain, seseo is considered "more socially acceptable or perhaps 'less substandard' than ceceo."

The following table gives an example of the three pronunciation patterns discussed so far:

	la casa "the house"	*la caza* "the hunt"
distinción	/la ˈkasa/	/la ˈkaθa/
ceceo	/la ˈkaθa/	/la ˈkaθa/
seseo	/la ˈkasa/	/la ˈkasa/

Special-Purpose Language and Skills in Spanish (e.g., traveling, careers)

- Buenos días: Good morning
- Por Favor: Please
- Señor, Señora, Señorita: Mr., Mrs., Miss
- Permítame que le presente a: Allow me to introduce you to
- Encantado: Delighted
- Gracias: Thank You
- De nada: You are welcome
- No hay de qué: Do not mention it
- Hasta la vista: So long
- El gusto es mío: The pleasure is mine
- Adiós: Goodbye
- Hasta mañana: See you tomorrow
- ¿Cómo está?: How are you?
- Está bien: It's all right
- En la estación de tren: At the railway station
- Pásame/déjame cinco dólares (tú): Pass five dollars to me
- Limpia tu cuarto (tú): Clean your room
- Salga del vehículo (usted): Exit the vehicle
- Váyase a casa (usted): Go home
- Entra a mi casa (tú): Come into my house
- Usa el computador (tú): Use the computer
- Llévame a un restaurante (tú): Take me to a restaurant
- Cómprate un vestido (tú): Buy yourself a dress
- Prepara el desayuno (tú): Cook breakfast
- Venga a mi casa (usted): Come to my house
- ¿Puedo entrar? (tú): Can I come in?
- Con permiso / Perdone: Excuse me

Knowledge of Linguistic Skills Necessary for Survival While Immersed in a Hispanic Cultural Situation

CURRENCY FROM SPANISH SPEAKING COUNTRIES

PAÍS	MONEDA
España	euro
Colombia	peso colombiano
Venezuela	bolívar
Ecuador	dólar estadounidense
Perú	nuevo sol
Bolivia	boliviano
Chile	peso chileno
Uruguay	peso uruguayo
Paraguay	guaraní
Argentina	peso argentino
Panamá	dólar estadounidense
Costa Rica	colón costarricense
Guatemala	quetzal
El Salvador	colón salvadoreño
Honduras	lempira
Nicaragua	córdoba
México	peso mexicano
Cuba	peso cubano
República Dominicana	peso dominicano
Puerto Rico	dólar estadounidense

Major Historical and Contemporary Developments in Spain and Latin America

Spain

Spain is a product of all the different civilizations that have invaded it and brought their own language and culture within. The Iberians of Mediterranean origin, were the first, followed by the Celts, who were of central European origin. Next, the Phoenicians from the north of Africa established colonies in the south of the peninsula. They were an advanced culture that introduced writing, metal works and the idea of using money into Spain. In the seventh century B.C., the Greeks established some colonies on the Oriental coast and introduced the cultivation of grapes and olives. The Carthaginians entered the peninsula in the sixth century B.C. They conquered the Phoenicians and acquired most of the peninsula. The Roman legions conquered the Carthaginians in 202 B.C. in what we know as the Punic Wars. The Romans stayed in Spain for six centuries during in which time they greatly shaped Spanish culture. They laid the foundation for the language, the law system, and the economic and social structures that remained. They built large aqueducts, bridges and many other public works. They founded cities and built schools, theatres and outdoor arenas. They also made Christianity and the Church as the more prominent way of life.

The Muslims began invading southern Spain in 711. They defeated the Visigoths, who then had control of the south. In 718, the Visigoths defeated the Muslims and regained control. Thus began a constant war between the Moors and the Christians that continued until 1492. Thanks to Arab influence, Spain became the most advanced and cultured country in Europe. The Moors brought their architecture, their art and their irrigation system. Córdoba (the Moorish capital) became a center for scholars from around the world to study math, science and medicine. In 1094, the Christians defeated the Moors in Valencia and Rodrigo Díaz de Vivar, known as "el Cid Campeador" ruled there until 1099 when he died after being defeated by the Muslims in Cuenca.

In 1469, Isabel, princess of Castilla married Ferdinand, prince of Aragón. She later became Queen of Castilla and he the King of Aragón. They became known as "Los Reyes Católicos" (The Catholic Kings). Together they defeated Boabdil, the last Moorish King in Granada. They reorganized the Inquisition and expelled the Jews from Spain.

Spain then became the first nation of Europe under the reign of "Los Reyes Católicos." To expand its territory Queen Isabel first agreed to help Christopher Columbus with his endeavor to the New World; others also helped expand the Spanish empire. Among these was Gonzalo Fernández de Córdoba, known as "el Gran Capitán." He conquered part of Italy in the name of Spain. During the reign of Carlos V (1517 – 1556), grandson of Ferdinand and Isabel, the Spanish nation acquired possessions in Germany, Austria, Italy, America, and North Africa. In 1556, Carlos V retired to a monastery and turned the empire over to his son, Felipe II, who ruled until 1598. Felipe's reign and its subsequent efforts to propagate Christianity saw the end of the Ottoman Empire in the Mediterranean and the incorporation of Portugal into the Kingdom of Spain after the death of King Sebastián, in 1578, to whom Carlos V was closely related. The destruction of its "La Armada Invencible" (The Invincible Armada), in 1588, by England, was a foreboding to the end of Spain's expansion into external territories.

Felipe II died in 1598 and his successors, Felipe III and IV, proved to be less than capable of ruling an empire of such great size. Spain suffered many losses of land. Spain was in economic ruin due to its countless wars, the immigration of its people to the New World and the expulsion of the Jews and the Moors.

The first Spanish republic established in 1873, lasted only 11 months. During this time, it passed through four presidencies. In 1898, by way of the Treaty of París, Spain lost possession of Cuba, Puerto Rico, the Philippines and Guam.

The second republic was declared in 1931, after Primo de Rivera, the previous dictator, was overthrown. It lasted only five years because of various political battles. During the second republic, Spain drafted a new constitution. The socialist republic that ensued then forced the king to flee and the right-wing's groups assumed the power of the general government, starting with a victory in parliament, in 1933. In 1936, "The Republican Popular Front," a right wing coalition with elements from the left, won the elections setting off a civil war between themselves and the insurgent Nationalist element of their government which was led by General Francisco Franco, who was assisted by both Italy and Germany in effecting his military coup. He defeated the republic's forces and established a dictatorship in 1939 that lasted until his death, in 1975. Soon after, King Juan Carlos became the new head of state. He began to dismantle the totalitarian apparatus and ushered in the democratic element of current Spanish government.

Indian Civilizations

Mayan – The most advanced of the Indian civilizations. They flourished from the third century to the sixteenth. The Mayans occupied what is now the Yucatán Península, Belize, Guatemala and parts of Honduras and El Salvador. They were a very advanced culture in science, astronomy and mathematics. They had made a calendar that managed to calculate with incredible accuracy, the duration of a solar year. They also had invented the numeral zero. They were also the only Indian civilization to create a system of writing to record influential events.

Aztec – They moved to the central Mexican valley in the twelfth century, remaining there until the sixteenth. They were an ambitious and religious people who had managed to conquer every tribe in the central Mexican valley and were still increasing their territory when the Spanish invaded them. They built large city-states and were the first civilization to practice mandatory education for all, regardless of gender or social status. All males were put in the army, from age seventeen to twenty-two and even peasants could rise to the rank of officer, if they worked hard enough. Their enormous capital, Tenochtitlán, with a population of 500,000, had causeways and canals surrounding it.

Inca – At the height of the Incan empire it was the largest empire on earth and remains the largest state to have ever existed in the Western Hemisphere. Cuzco, its capital "The Navel of the World," was the richest city in the New World. Their empire was located in the Andes and extended from Ecuador to central Chile, including parts of Bolivia and Argentina. The center of their nation was in Perú. They had an extensive political and social system. The Incans were also known for their royal family, well-organized army and system of roads. They spoke Quechua, a language that is still spoken in parts of Perú, Bolivia, Ecuador, and northern Chile.

Other Civilizations

In the Caribbean, at the time of Columbus's discovery of the Antilles, there were many Indian tribes living on those Islands that were similarly featured and related: the Arawaks, Taínos and "Caribes" or Carib.

In the mountains of Colombia, the "Chibchas" were the dominant civilization: a calm and religious people, famed for their expertise in their workings with gold and rituals, such as "el Dorado" (The Golden One), that revolved around it. Their works can be seen in the "el Museo del Oro" (The Gold Museum), in Bogotá. The "Guaraníes," in Paraguay spoke Guaraní, which is still spoken in certain parts of Paraguay. The "Araucanos" or "Mapuches" in Chile and Argentina, between the Bío Bío River and the Toltén River, were a warrior-tribe that resisted both the Incan Empires' and the conquistadors' advances.

Administrative Territories

In 1503, the "Casa de Contratación" (House of Trade), was organized in Seville, Spain as the centre for tax recollection and commercial regulation over the crown's property: such being the many colonies. In 1524, the Crown of Castille incorporated the new domains into the existing administrating organ of the "Consejo de Castilla" (Council of Castille), with Juan Rodríguez Fonseca as its head, resulting in the creation of the "Consejo de Indias" (Council of the Indies) and the "Real y Supremo Consejo de Indias" (Royal and Supreme Council of the Indies); priests and lawyers administered all colonies in America and the Philippines. Combining legislative, executive, and judicial functions under one organ of command it reported to the king weekly decisions over issues that would have been handled previously by the "Casa de contratación" (House of Trade). In 1680, the council's decisions were formally codified. In 1714, Borbón reforms enacted the creation of new posts: the "Ministro de Indias" (Minister of the Indies) and the "Secretario de Guerra, Marina e Indias," (Secretary of War, Navy and Indies), to assume the authority of the old council. The colonies were divided into four administrative territories. They were as follows: 1) New Spain, which included México, Central America, part of the United States and the Antilles, 2) Perú and Chile, 3) New Granada, which included Ecuador, Colombia, Panamá and Venezuela and 4) "Río de la Plata," which included Argentina, Bolivia, Paraguay, Uruguay and part of Brazil. A viceroy appointed by the king of Spain governed each.

The Spanish crown's principal objectives in colonization were to extend its economic, political, and religious empire by exploiting the natural resources of the indigenous cultures and civilizing the Indians through conversion to Catholicism.

Spanish Society

The Spanish society of the time was divided into four classes:

1) The Spaniards who governed.
2) The "criollos" (of Spanish origin but born in the colonies), who were well-off financially but could not govern.
3) The mestizos (the mixture of a Spaniard and an Indian), mulattos (the mixture of a Spaniard and a Black Slave), and zambo (the mixture of a Indian and a Black slave); who had neither social category nor political rights.
4) The native Indians and black slaves.

Independence

The inhabitants of the colonies grew tired of social and political injustice and of the economic restrictions placed on them by Spain. They were encouraged to seek their independence by three occurrences: the independence of the United States, the French Revolution, and the invasion of Spain by Napoleon's forces. There were four major revolutionary movements. These are:

México – In 1808, Napoleón installed his brother Joseph into the throne as the King of Spain. In the colony that consisted of modern day México, conservative criollos found their beliefs and values at odds with the liberal agenda of the newly installed French government and the local governors who adhered to its rule. Resistance sprang up and allegiance to the former King of Spain, Fernando VII, served as a spark for the "Grito de Dolores" (Cry of Dolores), beginning the Mexican revolution. Initiated on September 16, 1810, by Miguel Hidalgo, a priest at his own parish in the town of Dolores under the banner of the Virgin of Guadalupe, it attracted both followers and victory. The revolution, led by himself, his wife and his partner Ignacio Allende, marched towards Ciudad de México. Reaching the edge of the city, threatening to invade it, Hidalgo turned back and they were both eventually executed, in 1811. José María Morelos, a priest as well, became the new leader of the revolutionary movement. He occupied Oaxaca in November 24, 1812. He invoked the first Mexican national congress in Chilpancingo, Guerrero, in 1813. The Congress adopted a manifesto that elected him Generalissimo and granted him executive powers. He was about to possess his hometown of Valladolid (now called Morelia in his honor), but was defeated and hindered into retreat, leading to his execution, in 1815. He was apprehended by a royalist patrol led by a former follower. After losing its principal leader, Vincente Guerrero resurged as the new head of the revolutionary movement and was named protector of the independent Mexican congress. He moved the congress to Tehuacán and, in 1818, defeated General Armiso. This led to the announcement, in 1819, between himself and viceroy Apocada, to hold talks over an armistice between the government and the revolutionaries. As both sides came to the bargaining table, a coup was staged in Spain, in 1820 that changed the Spanish monarchy into a liberal institution, one that the central government in México disfavored. The general placed in command to quell the revolutionary movements' military force and set the terms for their surrender, Augustín de Iturbide, was pushed into total defeat and opted instead to offer his own version of a truce. In reconciling both opposing sides on Jan 20, 1821, under the "Iguala" plan –also known as the "Three Guarantees"–. The plan had three goals: establishing México as a country with the Roman Catholic faith as its one religion; proclaiming México as an independent nation; achieving social equality for every social and ethnic group within the country. That popularized it sufficiently with the revolutionary forces to give him enough momentum to form an alliance with them. The "Trigaranté Army" (Army of the Three Guarantees) was formed with the revolutionary armies and the government's troops under his own command, concluding the war for independence in México. He signed "The Treaty of Córdoba" on August 24, 1821, with Don Juan O'Donnojú, a Spanish replacement meant to be the new viceroy, assuring México as an independent empire from Spain and its own constitutional monarchy recognized by the Spanish throne. In the treaty, Iturbide was decreed First Chief of the Imperial Mexican Army and on May 18, 1822, following his rousing, a popular movement named him Emperor Augustín I. On March 19, 1823, he abdicated power after his opponents had grown too numerous.

They declared his disrespect of exercising power under the provisions of previous treaties and he was exiled to Italy. In 1824, he was executed after chasing the rumor of a possible Spanish invasion of México. Guadalupe Victoria, an old revolutionary, was named the first president of México, in 1824.

Nueva Granada (northern South America) – In 1808, Venezuela proclaimed its Independence from Spain and sent Andrés Bello, Luis López Méndez and Simón Bolívar to Great Britain on a diplomatic mission: a plan to foment full independence from Spain for all the colonies from the New World. On returning to Venezuela on June 3, 1811, he enlisted under the command of Francisco de Miranda, who acted as dictator of Venezuela, fighting with him until he was defeated and imprisoned by royalist forces. Simón traveled to Cartagena and wrote the Cartagena manifesto: he argued for the cooperation of all the different kingdoms of New Granada. He was persuasive and successful and he continued leading the revolutionary cause, invading Venezuela, taking the city of Merida and the capital, Caracas. There he was proclaimed "el Libertador" (The Liberator). He was defeated by the Royalists, in 1814 and found asylum in Nueva Granada where he intervened and assisted in freeing Bogotá after being appointed commander in chief of the forces of the federal republic. After falling out with province leaders, he sought refuge in Jamaica and there wrote the "Letter from Jamaica": a document on the current struggle and purpose of Latin American independence. He returned to Venezuela, in 1817, with assistance from newly independent Haiti and continued fighting. On August 7, 1819, Bolívar defeated the Spanish at the battle of Boyacá and founded "la Gran Colombia" (The Great Colombia) at the Angostura congress: it represented the now present-day areas of Venezuela, Colombia, Panamá and Ecuador. He was named president. His military hand: Antonio José de Sucre, Francisco Antonio Zea and Francisco Paula Santander, all kept fighting for a stronger and more independent state. Northern South America was completely liberated from all Spanish and royalist authority on May 22, 1822, when Antonio José de Sucre defeated the Spanish at Pichincha, in Ecuador. He began talks with the "Knight of the Andes," the liberator of southern South America, José de San Martín, to begin planning a total victory over the Spanish royalists. Eventually, Simón was made chief and defeated the Spanish in the battle of Junin on August 6, 1824 and the battle of Ayacucho on December 9, 1824. Spanish rule over South America no longer existed. On August 6, 1825, the Republic of Bolivia was created at the congress of upper Perú, which had been invoked by Antonio José de Sucre.

Perú and "el Río de la Plata" (southern South America) – In 1810, a momentous French invasion of Spain allowed for the wealthy residents of Argentina to seize power, asserting their own authority under King Fernando VII and deposing the viceroy. On July 9, 1816, the Argentine Declaration of Independence was signed. The connecting ties to the Spanish monarchy began their eventual separation. In the north remained the Royalist viceroy of Perú. Revolutionary movements, created to sever any possibility of Spanish rule, were starting to formulate.

The splintered factions looking for personal gain, which had earlier assumed authority, were now in a position to claim complete control. José de San Martín, a lifelong soldier and veteran of the Napoleonic wars, offered his services in 1812. In 1814, José de San Martín was appointed to command the Revolutionary Army. He later resigned and at the edge of the Chilean Andes and with the help of his longtime friend and Chilean patriot Bernard O'Higgins, enlisted support from the patriots residing in Chile and the Argentine government, raising an army: "el Ejército de los Andes" (The Army of the Andes). They crossed the Andes with success and defeated the Spanish on February 2, 1817, re-establishing a national government in Santiago, placing O'Higgins at the head as the Republic's first president. Chile was fully independent in April, 1818. After failing in negotiations with the Royalists, in Perú, upon Martín's suggestion that they themselves form an independent monarchy, Martín's forces began incursions into Perú and backed the remaining Spaniards into defeat, in 1821, as a result of blocking their last remaining seaport. José de San Martín was proclaimed the protector of Perú. In 1822, he abdicated his powers at the first invocation of the Peruvian congress and he then left them in Bolívar's hand.

Cuba – Cuba remained loyal to Spain until 1868, when Carlos Manuel de Céspedes began the freedom movement, with what was known as the "Grito de Yara" (Cry of Yara), to set Cuba free. This began a ten-year war waged by Cuban guerrillas, known as the Mambises and they fought with victory and acclaim. As Cuba prepared for its independence, José Martí, a famous poet and writer, started the Cuban Revolutionary Party.

In 1878, the remaining revolutionaries in Cuba signed the pact of Zajón, providing general amnesty for all combatants and freeing all slaves involved in the act. Yet, independence had not been reached and the United States had begun implementing its interests in expanding its reign over the small and treasured island. A small effort saw its initiation in Major Calixto García's and José Maceo's attempt at independence, called "la Guerra Chiquita" (The Little War). It was time for a renewed strategy. Calixto García, Antonio Maceo, Máximo Gómez and José Martí banded together most of the veterans alive from the ten-year war and set sail from Florida to fight in Cuba. Combat led to a stalemate with the Spanish, which the United States took advantage of, citing the precedent of the destruction of the U.S.S. Maine as a reason to engage Spain and annex Guam, Cuba, the Philippines, and Puerto Rico from them. Martí died in 1895, during an invasion to Cuba. Cuba became a republic in 1901.

Revolution

The development of Latin American nations after their independence from Spain varied from country to country and was influenced by several factors that all held in common and that resulted in different stages and degrees of statehood.
Arriving at a stable position in government conflict between bilateral opposing parties (Liberal and Conservative) and reaching a peace with guerrilla movements or the democratically transforming, authoritarian, repressive regime has been the end-in-sight for most Latin American nations in the 21st century.

The mixture of the lower classes and ethnic Indian groups into the governmental structure and the balance of foreign influence and encroachment were central causes for conflict and stagnation. Of those nations that did not sustain a democratic process, armed conflict between the government and its critical or armed opposition ensued in the form of armed and unarmed revolutionary movements, military coups and state-sponsored military repression.

México

After independence, México was involved in the Mexican-American war (1846-1848), with the United States, during Antonio López Santa Anna's reign over the then unsettled state of Texas, which eventually became part of the United States. In 1855, Ignacio Comonfort bridged the gap between Liberals and Conservatives by becoming the nation's first moderate president. In 1857, the newly enacted constitution left the exclusivity of the Catholic Church as México's sole religion unremarked and set off a bloody four year civil war that had liberals allying with moderates to stunt the conservatives' inclinations towards the Church's interest. The Liberals were the victorious ones, making Benito Juárez president. In the 1860s, México was invaded by France, which created the Second Mexican Empire under Habsburg Archduke, Ferdinand Maximilian of Austria. They were then overthrown and General Porfirio Díaz –the next president, aided by the United States. Their final victory on May 5, 1862, led by Ignacio Zaragoza, is the origination of the "Cinco de Mayo" celebrations. Porfirio Díaz inaugurated his presidency in 1876, through the Plan of Tuxtepec and remained in office for thirty years. His reign was called the "Porfiriato" because of its length and consistent production of public works aided by heavy foreign capital investment. The lower classes were systematically exploited and unrepresented in their motivations for social change. Francisco Madero intended to run against Díaz for the presidency in 1910 and was jailed by his opponent. He fled to the United States and initiated a revolt, with native Indians supporting him, which put him in power through the support of other opposition leaders such as Zapata, Carranza and the United States. Disagreements over the issue of land reform with Zapata, who had written the "Plan de Ayala," led to the loss of popular support and instigated a coup d'etat by his military commander, Victoriano Huerta, who executed him and his vice-president one week later. Other leaders disagreed with his station and issued the "Plan de Guadalupe," initiating a front-face conflict with him. Villa, Zapata, Carranza and Obregón fought him and forced him to flee to Puerto México; the United States invaded Veracruz and these predicaments led him to flee to Spain. Carranza became the next president and was deposed by Villa and Zapata –the former who became president in 1915. Carranza adopted a new constitution, becoming president in 1917 and was again deposed, in 1920, by Obregón. Carranza was assassinated in 1920. He had assassinated Zapata in 1919. Villa was assassinated in 1923. Obregon's successor Plutarco Elías Calles, assumed the presidency in all but in name, in 1928, after his assassination. In 1934, the progressive General Lázaro Cárdenas was elected president and in the following four decades coined the term "El Milagro Mexicano" (The Mexican Miracle) because of the nation's industrial rise and social advancement.

República Dominicana

The República Dominicana was occupied by Haiti for twenty-two years after their independence from Spain. They became free again, in 1844, after Pedro Santana's military force expelled the invaders. He volunteered the Dominicans back into the Spanish Empire, in 1861 and following a rebellion to this measure the Dominicans restored their independence, in 1865. The United States ruled the República Dominicana, in 1916-1924, through a military government. The first elected president, in 1924, was Horacio Vásquez. In 1930, Rafael Trujillo, a prominent army commander ousted President Horacio Vásquez and established absolute political control as dictator. He modernized the nation through many public works, but his repressive regime fell hard upon any critics of its rule. He massacred twenty thousand Haitian sugar cane workers in a response to the Dominicans working in Haiti, across the border, to overthrow him. After trying to form a plan to assassinate the Venezuelan President Rómulo Betancourt his government was singled out and acted against by the Organization of American States (OEA) and the United States. He was assassinated by his own troops. His son Ramfis Trujillo was president for a short while, but was then exiled as Joaquín Balaguer came into power. He resigned in 1962, and a council under President Rafael Bonnelly held power, until 1963, when Juan Bosch of the "Partido Revolucionario Dominicano" (PRD or Dominican Revolutionary Party) was inaugurated president. He was overthrown by a right-wing military coup in 1963. A civilian triumvirate adopted a joint dictatorship, until 1965, when military elements vying for Bosch's return and the proponents of a new general election came to a head –anti-Bosche forces calling in the United States for assistance. In 1966, Balaguers' Reformers Party had him assume the presidency, as well as in 1970 and 1974. He was defeated by Antonio Guzmán Fernández in the 1978 election, marking the first peaceful transfer of power to an opposing party in the nation's history.

Cuba

After becoming a possession of the United States, the Republic of Cuba gained formal independence on May 20, 1902, with independent leader Tomás Estrada Palma becoming the country's first president. In 1906, a revolt in Cuba led to United States intervention –as was specified in their special amendments to the Cuban constitution. In 1908, José Miguel Gómez was elected president and power was transferred back to Cuban control. In 1925, Gerardo Machado y Morales suspended the constitution and made himself Cuba's first dictator. In 1933, a military coup deposed him and installed Carlos Manuel de Céspedes –not the same from the Cry of Yara, as Cuba's new leader.

Later that year, Sergeant Fulgencio Batista overthrew him and replaced him with Carlos Mendieta y Montefur. Aiming for Cuban sovereignty, Batista himself ran for president, in 1940, but was opposed by the leader of the constitutional liberals Ramón Grau San Martín. He turned instead to the Cuba's Communist Party, which eventually generated his election. Grau became president in 1944 and Carlos Prío Socarrás of the same party, in 1948. In 1952, he staged a coup –for he had slim chances of winning– and became dictator. In 1956, Fidel Castro and a group of young nationalists sailed to Cuba, on a boat called "Granma" from México and began their insurrection in the Sierra Maestra Mountains. Batista fled in 1959 and Fidel assumed power that has lasted to this day. Osvaldo Dorticós Torrado became president in 1959, as Fidel was the first secretary of the communist party. In 1976, a new constitution was introduced that made him president, while still remaining chairman of the council of ministers.

Costa Rica

In 1838, Costa Rica proclaimed itself a sovereign and independent nation from its prior allegiance to "The United Provinces of Central America": consisting of the areas of Guatemala, El Salvador, Honduras and Nicaragua under the rule of Braulio Carrillo. In 1856, William Walker, a United States explorer bent on conquering Central America and claiming it to be part of the United States, invaded Costa Rica, but he was repelled by the national army. In 1899, the first democratic elections were held under peaceful auspices. In 1917, Federico Tinoco Granados ruled as dictator and was ousted, in 1919. In 1948, José Figueres Ferrer led an armed uprising to challenge the recent and questionable elections. In 1949, he abolished the army after two thousand casualties came out from a forty-four day civil war.

Guatemala

Rafael Carrera was the leader who broke Guatemala away from "The United Provinces of Central America." He ruled until 1865. Starting his presidency in 1871, Justo Rufino Barrios was the leader of the country's trend in modernization and also fought to reunite the Central American provinces. He was killed on the battlefield, wanting to achieve this, in 1885. Manuel José Estrada came into power in 1898 and invited the United Fruit Company to do business with the country. A coup d'etat in 1920 installed General José Orellana into the presidency. In 1931, Jorge Ubico, a member of the Progressive party, was unanimously elected president and he recognized himself as dictator. In 1944, his office was overthrown by the "October Revolutionaries," lead by Jacobo Arbenz and Francisco Javier Arana. A general election chose Juan José Arévalo as president in 1945. Arana was killed in a failed coup, but Arbenz managed to succeed Arévalo in a general election in 1951. The United States orchestrated a coup against his communist aligned government and Colonel Carlos Castillo Armas assumed power. He was assassinated in 1958, and General Ydígoras Fuentes assumed power. In 1960, a group of junior officers began their own rebellion, which was stammered and led to their extending ties with Cuba. In 1966, President Julio César Méndez Montenegro began counter-insurgency operations in the countryside.

The Guerrilla Army of the Poor (EGP), the Revolutionary Organization of Armed People (ORPA), the Rebel Armed Forces (FAR), and the Guatemalan Labor Party (PGT) all battled against the government and joined together as the Guatemalan National Revolutionary Unit (URNG), in 1982. Right-wing groups such as The Secret Anti-Communist Army (ESA) and The White Hand, battled the civilian population whom they identified as possible perpetrators and enemies. In 1982, junior officers willing to prevent the ascension of General Ángel Aníbal Guevara as president staged a coup d'etat. General Efraín Ríos Montt was elected. He promptly annulled the 1965 constitution, dissolved Congress, suspended political parties and cancelled the electoral law. He began forming local civilian defense patrols (PACs) and the resulting imbroglio constituted a mass genocide of the rural and Indian population. He was deposed, in 1983, by General Óscar

Humberto Mejía Victores, whom allowed a return to democracy and a new constitution to be drafted, in 1985.

Honduras

Honduran Francisco Morazán became the president of "The United Central American Provinces" in 1830 and upon its dissolution, in 1838, intended to reunite them through force. He was ousted by General Francisco Ferrera, who became president in 1841. Morazán was executed in Costa Rica in 1842. United States soldier of fortune William Walker intended to invade, but was captured by the British and executed in Honduras, in 1860. Internal conflict between liberals and conservatives was swayed by the influence of like-minded-parties in neighboring Guatemala, El Salvador and Nicaragua. The United Fruit Company shipped its first shipment of bananas from Honduras and so became its center of exploitation. In 1899, the peaceful transfer of power from Liberal Policarpo Bonilla to General Sierra marked the first constitutional shift of power. After him, Manuel Bonilla assumed power and set the foundation for the "Partido Nacional de Honduras" (National Party of Honduras or PNH), which exists to this day. In 1956, a coup d'etat, led by the former president's son, ousted Lozano Díaz, then current president. The military dissolved congress in 1963 and assumed power. Suazo Córdova was the first civilian elected president in ten years, in 1981.

El Salvador

In 1823, El Salvadorian Manuel José Arce formed "The United Central American Provinces." In 1832, Anastasio Aquino led an indigenous revolt against criollos and mestizos. In 1838, El Salvador became independent after "The United Central American Provinces" dissolved. General Maximiliano Hérnandez Martínez came into power during a coup, in 1931, and embraced a brutal oppression of all resistance movements. Farabundo Martí's peasant uprising, in 1932, was decimated into "La Matanza" (The Massacre). The National Conciliation Party held power from the early 1960s, until 1979. In 1967, Fidel Sánchez Hernández became president and manned the helm during the brief "Soccer War," against Honduras. In 1972, José Napoleón Duarte, opposing military rule, ran for president and lost. An ensuing coup d'etat to impose his own rule led to his exile. Leftist guerrilla groups began to form and total war erupted in both the cities and the countryside. Right-wing death squads began to kill indiscriminately. The

Salvadorian Armed forces perpetrated the "El Mozote" massacre. In 1979, the Revolutionary Government Junta, a group of military officers and civilian leaders, ousted the president's and General Carlos Humberto Romero's right-wing government. In 1980, the murder of Archbishop Óscar Arnulfo Romero, whom had asked for the United States to stop granting aid to El Salvador's armed forces, led to a new constituent assembly. Álvaro Alfredo Magaña Borja was selected its provisional president. In 1980, all left-wing guerrilla groups coalesced into the Farabundo Martí National Front (FMNL). After drafting a new constitution, in 1983, Duarte was elected president, in 1984. In 1989, the Nationalist Republican Alliance's (ARENA) Alfredo Cristiani became president and marked the first time a switch within political power, between opposing sides, occurred without violence. After FMNL led an attack on the capital, San Salvador, in 1989, the FMNL and the government were invited to peace talks with the UN, eventually leading to the Chapultepec Peace accord and a cease-fire in 1992.

Nicaragua

Nicaragua separated from "The United Central American Provinces," in 1838. In 1853, Conservative General Fruto Chamorro took over the government and exiled the liberals who previously held it in control. A civil war ensued. William Walker assumed power later, in 1856. In 1857, a constituent assembly convened and named General Martínez as president. A revolt, in 1893, ousted Roberto Sacasa. General José Santos Zelaya, the man who initiated the revolt, was eventually called to be President. In 1926, General Emiliano Chamorro forced previous president Carlos Solórzano from power. The "Ejército Defensor de laSoberanía de Nicaragua" (Army for the Defense of Nicaraguan Sovereignty), under Augusto César Sandino, fought against social inequality. Anastasio "Tacho" Somoza García established a military dictatorship, in 1937, after assassinating Sandino –whilst in negotiations about the possibility of a peace accord. Leonardo Argüello was named president in 1947 and then replaced, through Somoza's handywork, by Benjamín Lacayo Sacasa. Somoza was assassinated in 1956 and was succeeded by his son. The "Frente Sandinista de Liberación Nacional" (Sandinista National Liberation Front), a student activist group, was created in 1961. In 1972, a three-man junta ruled the government. Following a Sandinista revolution, Dictator Anastasio Somoza Debayle was deposed and they took control of the government, in 1979. The United States granted aid to former National Guard members, organized and called "contrarrevolucionarios" (counterrevolutionaries or contras), starting in 1981. Daniel Ortega was sworn in as president, representing the new government, in 1985.

Panamá

Panamá seceded from Colombia, in 1903, with support from the United States, brought on by the upper circles' desire to govern independently. Liberal and Conservative parties were organized and arrayed to govern. A revolutionary junta controlled the government. In a 1969 coup d'etat, General Omar Torrijos assumed power. He died in a plane crash, in 1981. General Manuel Noriega assumed governmental control. He annulled the elections, in 1989, that elected Guillermo Endara to power. Noriega was overthrown by the United States and left Endara in control.

Colombia, Venezuela, Ecuador

In 1830, "La Gran Colombia" (The Republic of Greater Colombia) broke away into separate states: Venezuela, Quito (now known as Ecuador) and "Nueva Granada" (New Granada – is now Colombia and Panamá) in which Bolívar became president. In 1850, the "Partido Liberal" (The Liberal Party or PL) and the "Partido Conservador" (The Conservative Party or PC) were created and a Federalist-Nationalist friction was set into being. In 1853, the elected,Liberal president was deposed in a coup d'etat by General José María Melo. Melo dissolved Congress and named himself dictator, in 1854. His term lasted for eight months and was followed by conservative rule. In 1857, PC candidate Mariano Rodríguez adopted a new constitution and renamed the country the "La Confederación Granadina" (Grenadine Confederation). In 1861, Conservative President Bartolomé Calvo was deposed by liberals led by General Mosquera. He drafted the constitution of Ríonegro, in 1863, lasting until 1886. He renamed the country "The United States of Colombia." Mosquera was ousted and exiled in 1867. The federalist trends within the previous constitution were remade into a centrally organized political system in the new constitution of 1886, put into place by nationalist opposition candidate Rafael Núñez. Disenchanted liberals began "La Guerra de los Mil Días" (The Thousand Day War) with the Conservative government. They eventually signed a peace agreement, in 1902. Panamá seceded from the country, in 1903. General Rafael Reyes became president, in 1904. He replaced Congress with a National Assembly. In 1930, Liberals took charge of the government through their first elected president in many years, Enrique Olaya Herrera. The current reformist policy encountered resistance and in 1946, the PL's candidate, who differed with previous policy, spurred Gaitán –a popular reformist, into running independently. In 1948, he was murdered –over an unrelated incident and riots ensued throughout the capital destroying much of its downtown area in an incident called "El Bogotazo." "La Violencia" (The Violence), a period of undeclared war between liberals and conservatives, claiming two hundred thousand lives over the next ten years, followed. In 1949, Congress was closed by Mariano Ospina and General Rojas Pinilla assumed power through a coup d'etat, in 1954. An alternating system of government was set in place called "El Frente Nacional" (The National Front). One term was to be assumed by a Conservative candidate and the next one by a Liberal candidate. Alberto Lleras Camargo was the first president –a Liberal, elected on the basis of the previous accord. During this period, any opposition to the current agreement had no outlet in government and various guerrilla groups formed: "Ejército de Liberación Nacional" (National Liberation Army or ELN), "Fuerzas Armadas Revolucionarias Colombianas" (Armed Colombian Revolutionary Forces or FARC), "Ejército Popular de Liberación" (Popular Liberation Army or EPL), which were all based in communist ideology. In 1974, the National Front ended and Alfonso López Michelsen became president, in a peaceful change of power.

Venezuela separated from "La Gran Colombia" (Republic of Great Colombia), in 1830. General Páez was elected under the new 1830 constitution. In 1846, Páez selected liberal General José Tadeo Monangas as his successor and was exiled alongside every other conservative in the country. In 1858, almost all local caudillos (local leaders) were involved in "La Guerra Federal" (Federal War). General Juan C. Falcón was elected president after the war's termination. Antonio Guzmán Blanco established a dictatorship in 1870, centralizing the government. Later, in 1945, a coup d'etat placed Rómulo Betancourt in power, which led to constituent assembly elections, in 1946. The elected President in 1948, Rómulo Gallegos, was overthrown by the military and along with prior coup leaders, sent into exile. A three-man military junta was put in control of government, and the 1936 traditionalist constitution replaced the recent 1947 draft. Dictator Pérez Jiménez was forced to abdicate, in 1958. A five-man provisional military junta was formed and invoked a general election, in 1959. Rómulo Betancourt was elected president. The "Fuerzas Armadas de Liberación Nacional" (Armed Forces of National Liberation or FALN) surfaced in the 1960s, as a left-wing opposition group. Raúl Leoni proved, in 1964, to be the first Venezuelan democratically elected leader to receive previous office while remaining at peace.

Ecuador separated from "La Gran Colombia" (Republic of Great Colombia), in 1830. Gabriel García Moreno unified the country under the Roman Catholic Church, in 1865. He was assassinated in 1875. In 1895, the "Partido Liberal Radical" (Radical Liberal Party) came to power and reduced the power of the clergy, ushering in a liberal plutocracy. In 1941, an Amazonian border dispute with Perú led to a war where Perú won, annexing two hundred thousand kilometers of its territory. In 1972, a nationalist military regime seized power. In 1979, Ecuador returned to constitutional democratic rule under President Roldós.

Perú and Bolivia

Independent Perú's first President was Simón Bolívar. General Andrés de Santa Cruz y Calahumana marched into Perú and imposed a Perú-Bolivia confederation, in 1839. General Marshal Ramón Castilla assumed power, in 1845. In 1872, the first elected civilian president came to power: Manuel Pardo, leader of the "Partido Civilista" (Civilian Party or PC). General Andrés Avelina Cáceres assumed power, being elected president, in 1886. José Nicólas de Piérola overthrew him, through the "Revolución de 1895" (1895 Revolution), and assumed power. Colonel Oscar Raimundo Benavides seized governmental power, in 1914. Augusto B. Leguía y Salcedo assumed the presidency through a preemptive coup d'etat, in 1919. He was overthrown, in 1932, by the military and died in prison. The "Alianza Popular Revolucionaria Americana" (American Popular Revolutionary Alliance or APRA) founded in México, in 1924, was brought by Haya de la Torre, into Perú. In 1931, Sánchez Cerro was elected president, beating APRAs' Haya de la Torre. He was assassinated in 1993. The military overthrew the government, in 1948. They installed General Manuel A. Odría as president; the "Partido Demócrata Cristiano" (Christian Democratic Party or PDC) and "Acción Popular" (Popular Action or AP) were then newly created democratic organs. Haya de la Torre returned from exile in 1962, and upon winning the elections, was ousted by the military, led by General Ricardo Pérez Godoy who held a provisional junta for one year. Fernando Belaúnde, a member of the PDC, was president after the junta re-convened elections, in 1963. General Vásquez Alvarado overthrew the government, in 1968. Elections were held, in 1978, for a constituent assembly and the drafting of a new constitution. Former President Belaúnde was re-elected, in 1980.

Guerrilla group "Sendero Luminoso" (Luminous Path or SL) was spawned, in 1980, by philosophy professor Abimáel Guzmán Reynoso and the "Movimiento Revolucionario Túpac Amaru" (Túpac Amaru Revolutionary Movement or MRTA) was created in Lima.

Chile

Bernardo O'Higgins was Chile's first president after independence from Spain. The "Partido Liberal" (Liberal Party or PL), "Partido Conservador" (Conservative Party or PC) and "Partido Nacional" (National Party or PN) were created in 1857. Congress led a revolt against President José Manuel Balmaceda Fernández, in 1891 and assumed power. He later committed suicide in Argentina. President Alessandri Dipalma was deposed by the military, in 1924 and then reinstated by supporters led by Carlos Ibáñez del Campo and Marmaduke Grove Vallejo, in 1925. The "Frente de Acción Popular" (Popular Action Front or FRAP) socialist party was spawned, in 1958. In 1973, leftist UP (Popular Union or Union Popular) President Salvador Allende was either murdered or committed suicide after his government was ousted in a military coup d'etat, led by General Augusto Pinochet Ugarte, who established a dictatorship. Chileans elected Christian Democrat Patricio Ailwyn as interim president, in 1989.

Argentina

Bernardino Rivadavia was the first president of the Republic of Argentina, within the "Provincias Unidas de el Río de la Plata" (The United Provinces of the River Plate), in 1826. General Juan Manuel de Rosas established a dictatorship, in 1835. Rosas was overthrown by General Justo José de Urquiza, who called a constituent assembly and promulgated a constitution, in 1853. In 1930, General José F. Uriburu ousted President Hipólito Irigoyen. President Ramón S. Castillo was overthrown, in 1944, by army colonels, led by General Juan Perón. He was victorious in the 1946 election and established a dictatorship. The "Revolución Libertadora" (Liberating Revolution) ousted him, in 1955 and placed an interim government in power, under General Eduardo Lonardi. He was deposed and General Pedro Aramburu assumed power, in 1955. General Juan Carlos Onganía was deposed in 1970 and General Roberto M. Levingston was made president. Perón, returning from exile, in 1973, was elected president and died one year later. His wife María Isabel Perón, the vice president, assumed power. She was deposed in 1976 by the "Proceso de Reorganización Nacional." a military junta under the leadership of Jorge Rafael Videla. In 1983, Raúl Alfonsín was elected president.

Geographic Features and Influences in Spain and Latin America

Spain

Spain is agriculturally diverse. In the north, wood and fish are plentiful. In the central region, wheat and similar grains are harvested. The south is the birthplace of famous wines and olive oils; rice; the famous Valencia oranges; lemons; dates and other tropical fruits can be found in the southeast. The machinery, motor vehicle, and foodstuff industries are an important source of revenue. Spain is the eighth largest economy in the world.

Spain is temperate, although affected by various physical differences. The northern coast and mountainous region to the northwest are the coldest and has the most rainfall in the country. The south is warm. The central and southeast regions experience extreme climates: high temperature and dry heat in the summer and intense cold in the winter.

Administratively, Spain, including its possessions is divided into 15 regions; the north, which consists of Galicia, Asturias, Cantabria, El País Vasco, Navarra and La Rioja; the central region, which consists of Castilla, Madrid and Extremadura; the south, which consists of Andalucía; the east, which consists of Cataluña, Valencia, Murcia and Aragón. Each region is unique in its traditions, culture and in some cases its language. It would behoove the individual studying Spanish to research these in greater detail.

Major Cities

Madrid is the capital of and largest city in Spain. It has many places of historical interest like "el Museo del Prado," where one can find an impressive collection of works by great Spanish painters like El Greco, Velázquez and Goya; "el Palacio Real," one of the biggest and most luxurious palaces in the world; el "Parque del Buen Retiro," former recreational area for Spanish nobles; "la Puerta de Sol," the center of all Spain's highways.

Barcelona is the capital of Cataluña and Spain's principal seaport. The city is divided into two parts by "Las Ramblas," one of the most beautiful avenues in all of Europe. Barcelona has always been considered Spain's big artistic and cultural center.

Sevilla is the main city in Andalucía. The Cathedral of Sevilla is the largest gothic cathedral in the world and there one can find the tomb of Christopher Columbus.

Valencia is a port city on the edge of the Mediterranean and a large agricultural, industrial and commercial center.

Granada is situated at the foot of the Sierra Nevada. It was the Moor's last Spanish fort. El Albaicín is a place of interest because it is one of the largest tipsy villages in existence. La Alhambra, immortalized by Washington Irving in his book by the same name, and "el Generalife," another Moorish castle famous for its gardens are two other places of interest.

Córdoba was the governing capital of the Muslim empire and the most important cultural center in Europe in the tenth and eleventh centuries.

Toledo is located on the edge of the Tajo River. It was the residence of Spanish kings until 1560.

Cádiz is the Atlantic seaport.

Bilbao is the capital of Vizcaya and the industrial mining center of the north.

Burgos is the former capital of Castilla and León. There one can find the tomb of "el Cid Campeador," Spain's first national hero.

Santiago de Compostela is a city in Galicia visited annually by thousands of religious pilgrims. Legend has it that the tomb of the apostle Santiago, patron saint of Spain, can be found there.

Salamanca is the site of one of the oldest European universities, the University of Salamanca, founded in the thirteenth century.

* Even though, this is not as widespread as it used to be, in some places in Spain it is still customary to take a two-hour lunch break.

México and Central America

México is a rising industrial power in Latin America that has established industries in the fields of telecommunication, natural gas distribution and electric generation, as well as seaport and railroad construction. Its agricultural output mainly consists of the production of corn, beans, cotton and, potatoes. It is the world's major producer of silver, which produces close to one quarter of the total revenue of the economy. It is one of the world's leading producers of natural gas and petroleum. It has the seventh largest oil reserve in the world.

Its capital, Ciudad de México, was founded by Hernán Cortes on the ruins of Tenochtitlán, which was the former Aztec capital, in 1521. It has many points of interest. Among these: "el Paseo de la Reforma" (the most elegant avenue in the capital), "el Zócalo" (the major square), "el Palacio de Bellas Artes" (the largest theater in the country; which also contains a huge Mexican art collection), "el Museo de Antropología," "la Cuidad Universitaria," "la Basílica de Guadalupe" patron saint of México, "la Catedral," "Templo Mayo" (important ruins), the floating gardens on Xochimilco and the pyramids and temples of Teotihuacán. Other important cities: Guadalajara (principal center of agriculture and cattle raising), Veracruz and Tampico (important ports on the Golfo de México), Acapulco and Puerto Vallarta (famous beaches), Taxco (national monument of architecture and industrial center of silver) and Chichen Itza (ruins of former Mayan city).

México is considered, geographically, to be part of North America. It is the northernmost and westernmost country in Latin America. Its central region, which is the most densely populated in the whole country, is a great plateau that opens up to the north into dry and hot desert areas. The east and west feature two mountain ranges: the Sierra Madre Occidental and the Sierra Madre Oriental, which are outwardly surrounded by oceanfront facing lowlands. To the south, forest and tropical rainforest areas make up the land. The Tropic of Cancer divides the country into Tropical zones to the south and temperate zones to the north. Its northern border with the United States along the Río Bravo, or Río Grande, is the longest border in the world. The Isthmus of Tehuantepec is the southernmost point of North America and the northernmost point of Central America. It is the most populous Spanish speaking country in the world.

Guatemala

Guatemala's hot tropical climate permits for farming of various types of agricultural products. Its principal products are coffee, bananas and sugar. In the north are lowlands and in the south is a costal area where the majority of the population resides, the rest of the country being mountainous. Mayan languages are prominent in rural areas. Its capital is Ciudad de Guatemala.

Honduras

Honduras is historically an agriculturally producing country producing sugar, bananas and coffee. It recently has found a burgeoning textile and shrimp industry as a new source of revenue. The ruins of Copan are a point of interest for once being the center of Mayan civilization. Eighty percent of Honduras consists of mountains with plains along its costal area, lowland jungles in the northeast and a valley in the northwest, which is its most heavily populated area. The Negro River is its boundary with Nicaragua. Its capital is Tegucigalpa.

El Salvador

El Salvador has the second strongest economy in Central America with a thriving telecommunications, banking and textile industry. Coffee is its main agricultural product, but it also produces cotton and sugar cane. In El Salvador rest the Mayan ruins of Tazumal, Chalchuapa and San Andrés. It is the only Central American country without a coastline to the Caribbean Sea.

Two mountain ranges cross El Salvador from east to west: the Sierra Madre on the north and the southern range that is made up by volcanoes. It has a central plateau that consists of rolling plains resting between both mountain ranges. The plateau serves as the land for the majority of the country's population. There are narrow plains on its coastline with the Pacific. The Lempa River emptying into the Pacific Ocean is its only navigable river. El Salvador is the smallest country in Central America. It is known offhand "el pulgarcito de las Américas," (America's little thumb). Its capital is San Salvador. Nahuatl, an ancient Native American language, is prominent in all parts of El Salvador.

Nicaragua

Nicaragua is mainly an agricultural country producing corn, cotton, coffee, bananas and tobacco. It is the largest cattle raising country in Central America. It contains seven percent of the world's bio-diversity. It is the largest country in Central America. It has mountains in the north central region and lowlands adjoining the Atlantic and Pacific. One fourth of the country is protected as a natural park or biological reserve. The Masaya Volcanic national park is a point of interest. Its capital is Managua.

Costa Rica

Costa Rica's chief products for exportation are coffee and bananas. It also produces cocoa, sugar cane, potatoes and many types of fruit. Recently the fields of pharmaceuticals, electronics, financial outsourcing and software development have become main economic sources. Costa Rica is one of the oldest democracies in the Western Hemisphere. It is the only one that does not have an army. A civil guard maintains order. Costa Rica is home to five percent of the world's bio-diversity. The Corcovado and Tortuguero National Parks, as well as the Monterrey cloud forest are points of interest. Its capital is San José. Costa Rica is the only country in Central America whose population consists mostly of Caucasian people. Spanish is the first and most common language, but English is spoken often.

Panamá

Panamá's principal agricultural product is bananas, but the main source of its economy is banking and commerce. Its Colón free trade zone is the largest free trade zone in the Western Hemisphere. Panamá is the smallest populated Spanish-speaking country in the Americas. It is considered a land bridge between South and Central America. The Isthmus of Panamá is the dividing point where Central America ends and South America begins. Cristóbal is the terminus of the Canal Zone. Balboa is the port on the Pacific side. Its capital is Panamá City. Panamá is a melting pot; nine percent of its population is Chinese.

Bolivia

Bolivia has very rich mineral reserves that produce tin, copper, zinc, lead, sulfur and gold. It has the second largest natural gas industry in South America. It is a landlocked country that only has access to the Atlantic through the Paraguay River. Bolivia's population is concentrated on the western part: a great plateau called the "Altiplano," where half its population lives. East are grasslands and rainforests. Lake Titicaca, located between Bolivia and Perú, is the tallest commercially navigable lake in the world and South America's largest freshwater lake. Within the department of Potosí lies the "Salar de Uyuni," the world's largest salt flats. The country is named after Simón Bolívar. Its capital is La Paz: the capital with the tallest altitude in the world. Bolivia has the highest indigenous population ratio in all America. Spanish, Quechua and Aymara are all equally recognized in Bolivia.

Perú

Perú's mining industry produces copper, gold and other precious minerals for major source of its revenue. It has widespread agricultural sectors, with a variety of products for both domestic and foreign markets such as corn, cotton and different fruit trees. Fishing has always been a popular industry. In the north coast llamas, sheep and goat-like animals are kept. Cebu cattle roams, fit to the Amazonian climate. The Andes mountain ranges divide the country into three regions: the Pacific coast, which is desert-like; the sierra, which is dominated by the Andes and where more than half the country's population lies; the jungles of the Amazon, which cover more than sixty percent of the country. The

Sechura dessert is located in the northwestern area close to the Pacific coastline. The roots of the Amazon River are located in Perú. Perú is home to eighty-four of the one hundred and four remaining ecosystems on earth. The Manu National Park is the most diverse rainforest in the world. The mysterious Nazca lines are found within the coastal plains. Near the city of Cuzco one can find the ruins of Machu Picchu, a former Incan city. There one can also find the University of San Marco, the first university on the continent, founded in 1551. Lima is its capital and an agricultural and industrial center –originally a fishing village. The city of Arequipe, "la Ciudad Blanca" (The White City), is protected by UNESCO and is Perú's second largest city. Quechuais Perú's second official language.

Ecuador

Ecuador's main agricultural product is bananas, but petroleum is the economy's mainline. It also produces coffee, cacao, fine woods, flowers, shrimp and tuna. It has a complete range of geographical features that include islands, mountains, beaches and jungles. Most of the country's population is concentrated in the Pacific coast and in the central Andean sierra region. Cotopaxi, south of Quito, is the world's tallest active volcano. The Galápagos Islands, the site of Charles Darwin's inspiration for the "Theory of Evolution," are a point of interest.

Quito is Ecuador's capital and Guayaquil is its main port city. Cuenca is the center for the most part, of all the artisans who produce pottery, silver plates and gold work within the country.

Colombia

Colombia main products for exportation are: coffee –which it is world-famous for, topsoil, bananas and petroleum. It is the United States' largest exporter of flowers. It also produces carbon, gold, silver, platinum and emeralds. The Andes mountain range separates the country from the southeastern Equatorial border to the northwestern Venezuelan border. It separates into three mountain ranges, the "Cordillera Oriental," the east mountain range; the "Cordillera Central," the central mountain range; the "Cordillera Occidental," the west mountain range, all at the Colombian Massif. The Magdalena River runs to the coast and starts where the eastern and central mountain ranges separate. It is the country's principal river. East of the eastern mountain range are "llanos," extensive grasslands.

The Cauca River, which separates the central and western mountain ranges into a fertile valley, is the second largest river and one of the Magdalena's main affluents. The plateau in its central region and its extending basins are the country's most populated areas. There are lowlands west of the western mountain range and in the north, by the Caribbean coastline. The south is made up mostly of jungle and dense forest. Colombia is one of the most bio-diverse countries in the world. "Parque Tayrona" (Tayrona National Park), is a point of interest conjoining beaches, mountains and mountain forests. Bogotá is its capital and Medellín is its second most important city –it is the industrial nexus of coffee production and one of the fastest growing economic regions in South America. Cartagena is its principal commercial seaport and within it one can find intact colonial artifacts and architecture. It has many points of interest like: "la Ciudad Vieja" (The Old City), the old colonial city with colonial houses and churches; "La Muralla" (The Old Wall), a wall surrounding the city, bridled with cannons, that was utilized to protect it from English pirates; "El Castillo San Felipe" (San Felipe's Castle), a large castle built for the same purposes.

Venezuela

Venezuela produces coffee and cocoa. However, the agricultural industry is minimal –petroleum is the base of its economy. It has the world's seventh largest oil reserve. The northeastern extension of the Andes mountain range lies in the country's northwest region. Its population is concentrated in the mountainous regions of the east and in its coastal regions. The central region is made up of "llano," savannah and extends to the banks of the Orinoco, its main river and border with Colombia. The south, called the Guiana Highlands, is featured by mountain forest and jungle. Lake Maracaibo is the largest body of water in northern Venezuela and if considered a lake. It is connected to the Caribbean Sea by a fifty-four mile strait and is the largest body of water in South America. The world's tallest waterfall, "Salto Ángel" (Angel Falls), lies in the south. The "Cuevas del Guácharo" (Guacharo Caves) are Venezuela's largest and most magnificent caves. Caracas is both the political and commercial capital of the country. It is a modern city with beautiful streets and buildings.

The Antilles (group of islands in the Caribbean Sea)

Cuba

Cuba is of the main producer of sugar cane in the world. Cattle raising and fishing are also important industries, and the country is rich in mineral deposits. It also produces tobacco – known worldwide for its quality, nickel, rice and a large variety of fruits. Its organic agriculture initiative is noted for its innovation and the pharmaceutical industry is being heavily invested in.

Cuba is the largest island in the Caribbean and the last surviving communist state in Latin America. Cuba was the first of the Antilles to be discovered by Columbus on his first trip to the New World. It is known as the Pearl of the Antilles because of its beautiful countryside and beaches. Its capital is Havana. The Castle of "el Morro" is a place of great historical interest because it was a fort used to protect the island from pirates in the seventeenth century. Guantánamo is an American naval base located on the island.

República Dominicana

The República Dominicana's economy is based on agriculture. Its main products are sugar cane, cocoa, coffee, plantains and corn. Citrus, green vegetables, pineapples, and flowers have grown important. Fishing is also becoming a major industry. It also bears the world's largest open-pit gold mine. It has three mountain ranges: central, septentrional, and eastern, that cut the island from east to west. In the south, where most of the population concentrates, are rolling plains, while the west is arid and is made up of shrubs and cacti. The north side of the island is made up mostly of beaches. The República Dominicana occupies two-thirds of the island of Hispaniola, the other third is occupied by Creole speaking Haiti. Its capital is Santo Domingo. There one can find the first chapel, first hospital and first cathedral in the New World, as well as the New World's oldest university –Santo Tomás de Aquino University, known today as the University of Santo Domingo.

Puerto Rico

Puerto Rico's main staple is sugar cane. The petrochemical, pharmaceutical and technology industries are a rising addition to the current economy. It is mostly a mountainous island with coastlines on its north and south faces. The "Cordillera Central,"" the central mountain range, runs through the island. To the northwest lie beautiful beaches such as Jobos beach, María's beach, Domes beach and Sandy beach. The island came into possession of the United States, in 1898. Today it is known as a commonwealth. Its inhabitants have United States citizenship (since 1917). The island of Puerto Rico was discovered by Columbus, in 1493. The largest telescope in the world, the Arrecibo Observatory, is situated on the island. Its capital, San Juan, was established in 1508, by Ponce de León. It is an active commercial port and possesses beautiful and ancient forts from the Spanish Colonial era.

South America

Argentina

Argentina has a traditional, middle class economy that is largely self-sufficient. Livestock and grains are the country's major source of revenue. Its economy's famed products, its wines and meats, are recognized to be excellent by the rest of the world. Textiles, leather goods and chemicals are prominent products within the overall economy. It is the second largest country in South America and the seventh largest in the world. The "Tierra del Fuego" (Land of Fire) and Patagonia in the south are made up of grassland and thorny forests.

The Chaco, in the north and northeast, is made up of jungle, swamps, mountains and the Iguazú falls lie within it. The Pampas, the country's central fertile plains, are home to the majority of the country's population and agricultural industry. Buenos Aires, its capital, possesses one of the most active seaports in the world. It is a very sophisticated city with a triage of elegant avenues, stores and theatres. Its second most important city is Rosario, a port city and industrial center. German, Spanish and Italian immigrants make up most of the population with native Indians representing a small percentage of the total race makeup. It has the largest Jewish population in all Latin America.

Uruguay

Uruguay's principal industry is cattle. It is also one of the world's leaders in the production of cotton. Tobacco and sugar are agricultural staples. Textiles, soy bean, cement and lime are produced as well. Vegetable oils are a rising industry. It is the smallest Spanish-speaking country in South America. It is made up of rolling plains and hundred of miles of beautiful beaches along the coast. El Negro River bisects the country from east to west. Montevideo is its capital and major port.

Paraguay

Paraguay's economy is agriculturally based. Its most important products are tea leaves and wood. It is landlocked on both sides, east and west, but it has many navigable outlets to the River Plate estuary bordering the Atlantic Ocean. The Paraguay River cuts the country into two east-west sections. In eastern Paraguay, between the Parana and Paraguay rivers, is the country's largest concentration of people. The west is mostly made up of marshes, lagoons, dense forests and jungles. Its capital is Asunción and is also its major port. Guaraní is its other dominant language, besides Spanish.

Chile

Chile is the world's largest producer of copper and mineral ore. Its chief products are grapevines and cereals. It is the world's longest country. The southernmost point of South America Cape Horn; Punta Arenas, the southernmost urban area in the world; Easter Island, home to a mysterious ancient civilization; Patagonia, the polar south region adjoining Antarctica, are all points of interest. The central valley's rolling plains are home to the majority of the country's population and agricultural industry. The north region is the Atacama Desert, known as the driest place on earth. Its most important cities: Santiago, the capital; Valparaíso, the principal seaport and Viña del Mar, a famous beach.

*   *   *

Significant Dates

In 1826, Simón Bolívar made the first attempt to bring world leaders together. He invited representatives from all the nations of the New World to come together in Panamá. Though only four countries sent delegates, the Panamá Conference was still a success. The First International Conference was held in the United States (Washington, D.C.) in 1889 – 1890. Its purpose was to maintain peace and better commercial relations between countries. In the Conference of Buenos Aires, in 1920, the Pan American Union was created. Its purpose was to establish cultural and economic ties between 21 nations.

In 1948, the ninth Pan American Conference took place in Bogotá. The alliance was recognized and given a new name "Organización de Estados Americanos - OEA" (organization of American States). It is now part of the United Nations and has many functions. Some of these functions are: to maintain peace among its members, to mutually assist each other in times of need and to work towards cultural, social and economic progress.

The "Área de Libre Comercio de las Américas," (Free trade Area of the Americas), a United States initiative to reduce trade barriers, was initiated with NAFTA (North American Free Trade Agreement) with México, in 1994. It eventually aims to enact multiple TLCs' "Tratados de Libre Comercio," (Free Trade Agreements) with every nation in the American continent, except Cuba.

Famous Explorers

Cristóbal Colón – founded the first European colony in the New World in 1492. It is known today as Santo Domingo.

Juan Ponce de León – established a Spanish colony in Puerto Rico in 1508. He also discovered Florida in 1513 while searching for the Fountain of Youth.

Vasco Núñez de Balboa – located the Pacific Ocean in 1513.

Hernán Cortés – discovered destroyed the Aztec empire in 1521.

Fray Vásquez de Coronado – discovered the Grand Canyon while searching for the seven cities of "Cibola."

Álvar Núñez Cabeza de Vaca – explored most of Florida, the Mississippi and northern México.

Pedro de Valdivia – conquered Chile and defeated "los Araucanos." He also founded the city of Santiago, Chile in 1541.

Bartolomé de Las Casas – was a missionary known as "The Apostle of the Indians" or "Protector of the Indians" because he dedicated himself to making a better life for the Indians.

Fray Junípero Serra – evangelist who founded a series of missions in California.

* * *

Major literary figures, works, and movements of Spain

Alfonso X is the most prominent figure in Spanish literature of the Middle Ages. He brought together the most learned men of those times to translate and write texts on various subjects such as history and astronomy.

In the fourteenth century, cowboy novels began to appear. These satires described the supernatural adventures of its heroes. In the fifteenth century, poetry became popular.

Jorge Manrique is a famous poet who wrote poetry to honor his father. Henry Wadsworth Longfellow has translated his work into English.

Antonio de Nebrija is famous for having written the first Spanish grammar book.

The Golden Age is the most glorious era of Spanish literature.

Garcilaso de la Vega was a soldier and poet who truly represented the Renaissance. He introduced Spain to various new forms of poetry such as the sonnet.

Miguel de Cervantes y Saavedra is most famous for having written "Don Quixote," which is one of the world's most read books –printed in several languages. This is a satirical novel whose underlying message was the conflict between idealism and materialism. Cervantes was a soldier who lost the use of his left arm in a war. Pirates held him prisoner for five years. He was unlucky in both marriage and business, having spent years in prison because of a bad business deal.

Lope de Vega wrote all types of works but his most famous were dramas. It is said that he is the father of the modern comedy as well as the creator of the National Theatre of Spain.

This era also saw various other writers such as: Francisco de Quevedo, a satirical writer; Juan Ruiz de Alarcón, a Mexican whose plays put down vices, honor and virtue; Tirso de Molina, who was a Spaniard famous for having created Don Juan and Pedro Calderón de la Barca, whose plays deal primarily with honor.

In 1713, the Academy of the Spanish Language was created. Its primary purpose was to maintain the purity of the Spanish language. This era also saw the beginnings of romanticism.

José de Espronceda was a romantic poet who has been compared to Lord Byron.

Mariano José de Larra was a very famous critical essayist who wrote under various pen names. José Zorrilla is most famous for having written a drama based on Don Juan from a romantic perspective. Gustavo Adolfo Bécquer wrote many lyrical poems.

Romanticism was followed by idealism. Fernán Caballero is the creator of "costumbrista" novels. The purpose of these types of books was to criticize or make fun at the customs of certain regions.

Juan Valera presented a poetic vision of his home, the region of Andalucía. Benito Pérez Galdós is considered the most important Spanish novelists of the nineteenth century. He was a violent critic of religious intolerance and of social injustice.

Emilia Pardo Bazán introduced naturalism and established contact between European and Spanish literature. She wrote mainly about her home, the region of Galicia.

Armando Palacio Valdés was a popular novelist who wrote about the region of Andalucía and about the fisherman of Asturias.

Vicente Blasco Ibañez was popular not only in Spain but all over the world. He was a great defender of republican ideas and of individual freedom. He was imprisoned on several occasions because of his political ideas.

Generation of '98

Because of the War of 1898, Spain lost what was left of its colonial empire. In the wake of this disaster, a group of young, Spanish intellectuals got together to examine the cultural and spiritual state of their country. They called themselves, the Generation of '98 (*Generación del 98*)

Francisco Giner de los Ríos was a philosopher, professor, and great educator of intellectuals. He founded "La Escuela Libre de Enseñanza," which is a center of liberal ideas.

Miguel de Unamuno was a philosopher, a critic, a poet, and a novelist. One of his favorite topics was the gap that exists between faith and reason, and between lack of faith and the desire for immortality.

Ramón del Valle-Inclán was famous for the richness of his language. His prose can practically be called poetry.

In the world of theatre, Jacinto Benavente is a well-known name. This dramatist won the Nobel Prize for Literature, in 1922.

Ramón Menéndez Pidal was a very important Spanish scholar in the twentieth century. He wrote several studies on medieval language and literature in Spain.

Pío Baroja was the principal novelist of the "Generación del 98 ." His novels contain a lot of action.

José Martínez Ruiz wrote essays and novels. His works compare the old Spain to the modern one in a simple and natural language.

Antonio Machado was one of the most loved and respected poets of this century. His poems are short but deal with fundamental themes. He introduced Ruben Darío's modernism in Spanish poetry.

Gregorio Martínez Sierra was most famous for having created notable female characters in his works.

José Ortega y Gasset was a philosopher and essayist who sought to depict Spain's spiritual values and traditions.

Generation of '27

The Generation of '27 (*Generación del 27*) was an influential group of poets and writers that arouse in Spanish literary circles between 1923-1927, essentially out of a shared desire to experience and work with avant-garde forms of art and poetry. Their first formal meeting took place in Seville in 1927 to mark the 300th anniversary of the death of the baroque poet Luis de Góngora. Writers and intellectuals celebrated an homage in the *Ateneo de Sevilla*, which retrospectively became the foundational act of the movement.

Juan Ramón Jimenez is known as the creator of "pure poetry." He wrote his famous *Platero y yo* in 1917. He relocated to Puerto Rico where he resided when he was awarded the Nobel Prize for Literature, in 1956. Besides his many poems, he also wrote books in prose.

Federico García Lorca was a poet and dramatist who focused on folkloric themes and traditions. His theatrical work deals with human passion.

Jorge Guillén was known for writing "pure" poetry, which is poetry created from concepts and abstractions. He taught in many universities worldwide including Harvard and Wellesley College.

Vicente Aleixandre was an essayist and poet who received the Nobel Prize for Literature, in 1977. His poetry is romantic and surrealistic at the same time, with love as its central theme.

Alejandro Casona was a dramatist who left Spain and settled in Argentina.

Effects of the Civil War in the Literature of Spain

The Civil War in Spain had as profound an effect on literature as on daily life. Many writers were against the dictatorship of Franco and left the country to continue their writing in other countries. Some were incarcerated and condemned to die. After the Civil War a group of writers emerged who had experienced the atrocities of the war firsthand. Their writing reflected the influence of the war in their preoccupation with social problems and the economy.

Julian Marías is a contemporary philosopher and essayist. He has taught at the University of Madrid, Harvard, Yale, and the University of California in Los Angeles.

Camilo José Cela is the most famous contemporary Spanish novelist and short story writer. In 1989, he won the Nobel Prize in Literature. His famous novel La familia de Pascual Duarte was written in 1942. His writing possesses a mocking tone.

Antonio Buero Vallejo wrote plays that modernized and gave dignity to Spanish theatre.

Miguel Delibes is a novelist who using simple language gives the reader a picture of the reality of Spanish society and of the humble man.

Carmen Laforet won the Nobel Prize for Literature with a very controversial publication that dealt with the lack of spirituality in Spain after the war. She published her first novel *Nada* in 1944.

José Hierro is one of the most notable poets of the postwar era. His humanitarian poetry is deep without using imagery.

Alfonso Sastre is a dramatist who writes about society with the goal of sending a message to the public.

Juan Goytisolo is another important contemporary novelist. He presents the problems and uncertainties of the times in his writings.

Antonio Gala is a poet and dramatist who presents modern themes using historical characters.

Major Literary Figures, Works, and Movements of Latin America

Rubén Darío was a Nicaraguan poet who was known as the "Prince of Spanish Literature" or the "Father of Modernism" by other great Spanish writers. His poems are a mix of traditionalism, romanticism and the poetic substance created from fusing such themes.

Gabriel García Márquez is the foremost proponent of the literary style dubbed "Magic Realism": the casual meshing of supernatural and everyday events. He is a pioneer of the Latin American "Boom" and was given the Nobel Prize for Literature in 1982, for the novel "*Cien Años de Soledad*" (One Hundred Years of Solitude). He is Colombia's most accomplished author and writes extensively in novels, short stories, and articles on the history and the mosaic picture of its daily life.

Jorge Luis Borges is Argentina's most prolific writer. His intellectually based themes are written in the form of short stories that compound philosophy and the entire universe of its ideas.

Gabriela Mistral is a Chilean educator, poet, and diplomat whose wonderful works of poetry are conformed by contemplations of death, faith, and motherhood. She was Latin America's first Nobel Prize winner, receiving it in 1945 for literature.

Octavio Paz was a Mexican poet and writer, whose focus in his writings tended to the union of civil liberty and nature and its corresponding love. He is México's most prestigious poet of the twentieth century. He won the Nobel Prize for Literature, in 1990.

Pablo Neruda was a Chilean Poet who wrote poetry that's main theme is the historical power of Latin America and its reflection within its vitality and living soul. He was the Nobel Prize Laureate, in 1971.

Sor Juana Inés de la Cruz was a nun from México, famous for being one of the most prodigious scholars of all times. She wrote poetry and prose that affirmed women's strength and their individual rights.

Spanish and Hispanic Art and Music

Spain is rich in folkloric music. Flamenco is perhaps its most famous contribution. It comes from the region of *Andalucía* and is a mixture of Arab, gypsy and Jewish music of the fourteenth century. It consists of a song accompanied by guitar music and an improvised dance.

The traditional instrument of Spain is the guitar, both in traditional and modern music. For accompaniment, the tambourine and castanets are often used.

Spain has given the world music known as the *zarzuela*. It is a combination of music, song, spoken dialogue, choruses, and dance. The most famous composers of this type of music are Francisco Asenjo Barbieri and Tomás Bretón.

Among the four most famous Spanish composers are Isaac Albeniz, Enrique Granados, and Manuel de Falla. Albeniz composed operas and piano music. Granados also composed piano music. De Falla was the most famous Spanish composer of the twentieth century. He focused on orchestra music and also wrote a few ballets. The fourth was the blind composer, Joaquín Rodrigo with his famous *Concierto de Aranjuez.*

Spain has also given the world some famous instrumentalists. Among these, we find Pablo Casals, José Iturbi, Andrés Segovia and. Casals was one of the most famous violoncellists in the world. He left Spain, in 1939, because he was against the dictatorship of Franco. He settled in Puerto Rico and began an international music festival that is still held yearly in his honor. Iturbi was a pianist and director of a symphonic orchestra. He also acted in several Hollywood movies. Segovia was one of the most famous guitarists the world has ever known. Alicia de Larrocha is a famous contemporary pianist known for her interpretation of great Spanish composers, as well as other famous composers.

Victoria de los Ángeles, Alfredo Krauss, Plácido Domingo and José Carreras are famous Spanish operatic singers. Sarita Montiel, Julio Iglesias, Raphael, Camilo Sexto, Rocío Jurado and countless others are more contemporary Spanish singers.

El Prado is the most famous museum in Spain. It is located in Madrid. It features one of the world's finest collections of European art, from the 12th century to the early 19th century, based on the former Spanish Royal Collection. Founded as a museum of paintings and sculpture, it also contains important collections of more than 5,000drawings, 2,000prints, 1,000 coins and medals, and almost 2,000 decorative objects and works of art.

There are many famous Spanish painters. Domenico Theotocopoulos, known as *El Greco*, was born in Crete. He studied in Italy and later moved to Spain. He lived in Toledo, until his death. His work is characterized by religious undertones and by the way he lengthens his figures.

José de Ribera was born in Spain but spent most of his life in Italy. His work is characterized by its realism and also his use of light and dark. Francisco de Zurbarán painted religious works in a sober and religious way.

Diego Velázquez was the leading artist in the court of King Philip IV. He also painted portraits of other Spanish nobles. He was an individualistic artist of the contemporary Baroque period, important as a portrait artist. In addition to numerous renditions of scenes of historical and cultural significance, he painted scores of portraits of the Spanish royal family, other notable European figures, and commoners, culminating in the production of his masterpiece *Las Meninas* (1656).

Bartolomé Ésteban Murillo was a religious painter who painted things like the Immaculate Conception.

Francisco de Goya y Lucientes was the most famous painter of his time. He was a Spanish romantic painter and printmaker regarded both as the last of the Old Masters and as the first of the moderns. Goya was a court painter to the Spanish Crown, and through his work was both, a commentator on and chronicler of his era. The subversive and imaginative element in his art, as well as his bold handling of paint, provided a model for the work of later generations of artists, notably Mane and Picasso.

Ignacio Zuluaga drew realistic pictures of people of the times like toreadors and gypsies. José María Sert is famous for his murals that depict *Don Quixote*.

Pablo Picasso was born and educated in the Spanish province of Málaga, but spent most of his life in other parts of Spain. He began the style know as cubism, a style that rejects traditional perspective. Among his most famous works are the proto-Cubist *Les Demoiselles d' Avignon* (1907) and Guernica (1937), his portrayal of the German bombing of Guernica during the Spanish Civil War.

Joan Miró is one of the most famous representatives of abstract art combined with surrealism. His works are testament to his vivid imagination.

Salvador Dalí was a prominent Spanish Catalan surrealist. His works represent the creativity of his subconscious mind with detail and vision. Dalí was a skilled draftsman, best known for the striking and bizarre images in his surrealist work. His painterly skills are often attributed to the influence of Renaissance masters. His best-known work, *The Persistency of Memory*, was completed in 1931. Dalí's expansive artistic repertoire includes film, sculpture, and photography, in collaboration with a range of artists in a variety of media.

* * *

Latin American Art

When the conquistadors arrived in the early fifteenth century, they found a very advanced art form left behind by the Indians. They had made pyramids, palaces and temples. They had made statues of their gods out of gold and silver and had made jewelry out of precious stones. They had also made elaborate pottery. The Spaniards brought a religious form of art to the New World, which served to convert the Indians to Catholicism.

One of the most famous Mexican painters is Diego Rivera. He began his early career influenced by cubism and post-impressionism. In his twenties, he decided to dedicate himself to painting murals that represented political and social themes. His large wall works in fresco helped establish the Mexican Mural renaissance. His murals can be seen today decorating many public buildings in México.

José Clemente Orozco was also a Mexican muralist who depicted the Mexican Revolution in his paintings. He also painted the frescos of the Palace of the Arts in México City and can also be found in the United States in Dartmouth College.

David Alfaro Siqueiros was a Mexican painter famous for his expression of idealism. He was arrested several times for his political expressions.

Rufino Tamayo was a famous Mexican painter who depicted the happiness and tragedy of his country's history. He won many international art prizes and his paintings adorn famous public buildings like the National Palace of Beautiful Art and the Museum of Anthropology, both in Ciudad de México, and the UNESCO building in París.

Miguel Covarrubias, also Mexican, was famous both in his country and in the United States as a painter of caricatures. His drawings have been printed in several magazines.

Cesáreo Bernaldo de Quirós was an Argentinean impressionist whose paintings represented the life of a "*gaucho.*" His paintings depict the history of the "*Pampas.*"

Wilfredo Lam was a Cuban surrealist painter. His paintings contained Afro-Cuban elements. Some of his works are on display in the Museum of Modern Art in New York City.

Some other artists include: Emilio Pettoruti, an Argentinean cubist painter; Roberto Matta, a Chilean surrealist; Oswaldo Guayasamín, an Ecuadorian cubist; Alejandro Obregón, a Colombian abstract painter; Rómulo Macció, a vanguard Argentinean painter; Fernando Botero, a Colombian figurative painter; and Gerardo Chávez, a Peruvian surrealist.

Most Hispanic music is a conjunction of rhythms brought by African slaves to the Caribbean or native rhythms and melodies preexisting in various indigenous cultures transplanted to the Western instruments brought by the Spanish. *Salsa, Merengue, Calypso, Mambo, Cumbia* and *Vallenato* are mixed African and western musical genres that originated in Puerto Rico, Cuba, the República Dominicana, Honduras, Guatemala, El Salvador, Panamá and the coasts of Venezuela and Colombia. Inland in México, *Mariachi* and *Ranchera* music are original and popular musical genres. Within Perú, Colombia, Ecuador, Bolivia, Uruguay,

Paraguay, Chile and Argentina, the Andean music "*Música Andina,*" a genre representing native indigenous musical rhythms and melodies, is frequently played and listened to. In Argentina, the music of choice and the genre most listened to is *tango*: a song and dance form both classical and folkloric; it is a profound dance technique for couples to participate in. It is developed from the expression of Argentinian and Uruguayan folklore.

* * *

SPANISH PEDAGOGY

I. PLANNING

Stephen Krashen's Language Acquisition Theory

This theory states that acquisition and learning are two separate processes. Learning is to know about a language – formal knowledge; acquisition is the unconscious mind related activity that occurs when the language is used in conversation. Krashen embodies the following hypotheses in his theory:

A. Natural Order: Natural progression/order of language development exhibited by infants/young children and/or second language learners (child or adult).

Level I: Pre-Production Stage (Silent Period): Minimal comprehension, no verbal production.

Level II: Early Production Stage. Limited Comprehension; One/two-word response.

Level III: Speech Emergence Stage. Increased comprehension; Simple sentences; Some errors in speech.

Level IV: Intermediate Fluency Stage. Very good comprehension; More complex sentences; Complex errors in speech.

B. Monitor: Learning (as opposed to acquisition) serves to develop a monitor- an error detecting mechanism that scans utterances for accuracy in order to make corrections. As a corollary to the monitor hypothesis, language acquisition instruction should avoid emphasis on error correction and grammar. Such an emphasis might inhibit language acquisition, particularly at the early stages of language development.

C. Input: Input needs to be comprehensible. Input + 1/Zone of Proximal Development- Input/instruction that is just above the students' abilities. Instruction that is embedded in a meaningful context, modified (paraphrasing, repetition), collaborative/interactive and multimodal.

D. Affective Filter: Optimal input occurs when the "affective filter" is low. The affective filter is a screen of emotion that can block language acquisition or learning if it keeps the users from being too self-conscious or too embarrassed to take risks during communicative exchanges.

In addition, the Cultural Adaption / Cultural Shock cycle for students, upon introducing themselves to a new language and its culture is to experience the following:

1. Honeymoon: The sojourner is intrigued by the differences she or he perceives and is excited about everything.

2. Disintegration: The differences between the cultures lead to confusion, isolation and loneliness. New cultural cues are misread and withdrawal and depression can occur.

3. Re-integration: The new cues are re-integrated but even though the individual has an increased ability to function in the new culture, he rejects it and experiences anger and resentment and acts hostile and rebellious.

4. Autonomy: The person is able to see the differences between the two cultures in a more objective way, is able to deal with them and therefore feels more self-assured, relaxed and confident.

    Independence: The social psychological and cultural differences are accepted and enjoyed (ibid.). And the person is able to function in both the old and the new culture; he has achieved bi-culturality.

*   *   *

The Common European Framework for Reference of Languages

It provides a basis for the mutual recognition of language qualifications and is increasingly used in the reform of national curricula and by international consortia for the comparison of language certificates. Within it lie the competencies necessary for communication, the related knowledge and skills, and the situations and domains of communication.

L1/L2

The terms L1 (First Language) and L2 (Second Language) are interspersed across the methodologies of present-day language acquisition. The distinction has been made to recognize the difference between learning a second language (such as the case of an immigrant) and learning a foreign language (such as the case of one who wishes to learn a language separate from their mother tongue).

Apprehension from one language to the other varies with each separate case. This distinction serves to rationalize different approaches for the education of the student and teacher according to his or her previous knowledge of the language other than the one being taught. The choice of teaching in the language to be known or the language already known is a choice as much for the teacher as it is for the student: its use is to define the place of instruction and learning in development.

L1 can be used in translation as a teaching technique; students can research in L1; present in L2. Beginners favor receiving teaching in L1 in topics such as grammar and to contrast listening, reading, and giving commands; intermediate and advanced students typically do not prefer to spend time in L1 for such activities, preferring L2 at all times. L1 is useful in the procedural stage for setting-up pair and group work; sorting out an activity that is clearly not working; checking comprehension.

The negotiation of meaning is the theme that unifies technique into coherence with all other factors in the teaching and learning process. The instructors' proficiency in the target language (the target or language to be known) is taken into discretion and regulates development by accommodating a choice in one language or the other; rote is minimal.

Use of Computers and Other Technologies

Using computers and the Internet, students can access databases of topical information on grammar, vocabulary, and spelling, which are kept alongside exercises on comprehension and performance. They also serve as didactic forums for students and professors to have lessons or for participating in real life conversations and exchanges with native speakers in the target language. They serve the various Internet media outlets, available in the target language; displaying art, news, advertising, and literature in a relevant and readily accessible form. Compact and laser discs are used to supplement on-line content. Visual aids and mediums also predominate in the education of young children acquiring Spanish as a second language.

Today, the different web 2.0 technologies, such as blogs, wikis, and podcasts, are offering a variety of collaborative and individual opportunities for students to become the doers not the receivers of learning. Teaching and learning is being redefined with a lot of opportunities for sharing of learning and individualized instruction. Virtual classrooms and language-based media centers are used as all-inclusive sites for the student to acquire Spanish or any other second language. They are available to students of all levels.

* * *

II. TEACHING

Listening Comprehension Approach to Language Learning

In the late 1960's, James J. Asher developed his listening comprehension approach to language learning. The students acquire receptive skills through intensive practice by listening and physically reacting to the message they hear. They are not required to produce spoken language until they have physically responded to the input. The instructor uses gestures, actions, and commands throughout the class. New material is interwoven with the old material. The input is constant and is constantly varying so it is not a repetitive drill. Students are walking, standing, pointing and are in a non-threatening environment.

Natural Approach

Tracy D. Terrell developed his Natural Approach Theory of acquiring a second language in the 1970's based in part upon Stephen Krashen's acquisition versus learning theories and his Input Hypothesis. The natural approach is cooperative and the underlying premise is that acquisition occurs when:

- The focus is on the content of the message and not the form of the utterance.
- The input is comprehensible.
- The learner is in a low anxiety environment (students see the teacher as an enabler and not as an authoritative figure; input is student-centered).

The instructor maintains the target language throughout the class by modifying their speech somewhat, using TPR and pictures. Students study rules and practice drills at home. The class time is devoted to introducing enough vocabulary and structure to participate in communicative activities where meaningful language is exchanged. Students work in pairs or small groups. Peer correction is encouraged; students encourage and support each other.

Audio-Lingual Method

The audio-lingual approach to language learning was generated by the U.S. Defense Forces language programs during and after World War II and is based on the stimulus-response theory of the American school of behaviorist psychology. It is considered an interdisciplinary approach.

The Audio-lingual Method (ALM) of the 1960's was based upon student memorizing phrases and sentences, patterning the teacher through endless drills in class. It was thought that the learner would develop good habits by constantly hearing and producing the sentences from the text. Dialogues were memorized, recited, and practiced. Structured and patterned response drills characterized the class.

The audio-lingual approach to listening emphasizes first listening to pronunciation and grammatical forms and then imitating those forms by way of drills and exercises. The manipulation of structures is the main focus of the Audio-lingual Method.

Grammatical Method

The grammatical method presents grammatical forms and patterns as exercises that are listened to, repeated and varied in a series of drills. It relies heavily on reading and translation, mastery of grammatical rules and accurate writing. It is predominately interpretive. The traditional Latin and Greek classroom of the late nineteenth and early twentieth centuries used this approach. Students study explicit grammar rules and bilingual lists of vocabulary words pertaining to a work of literature. Grammar and comprehension were tested throughout means of translation. The only speaking involved students conjugating verbs and reading literary passages aloud.

Communicative Approach

The communicative focus, using the task based method, introducing cultural and intra-cultural learning, is the current up-to-date technique for teaching proficiency in a second language. It emphasizes the use of "real" language, in real life situations, within a working frame from where it is naturally conveyed in everyday terms. It maintains a focus centered around the 4Rs:

READING
WRITING
CONVE**R**SATION
CULTU**R**E

Students are instructed to complete tasks that identify with the day-to-day communication that language use conforms to in social settings (ordering food, asking for directions, talking with friends, reading newspapers or magazines, singing songs or listening to music, watching movies or television, applying for a job, discussing current events, organizing social events, etc...). The teacher becomes a facilitator. Collaborative learning and peer interaction is important. Students and teachers select and organize curriculum contents. Mementos are created through the accomplishment of tasks personally and interpersonally related to real world language use.

The presence of another language's native speaker, attached as a full time personal conversational aide, is a new feature for acquiring a second language. It allows full access to real time input that is correlated to the student's immediate doubts about acquisition and his or her context in the frame of communication.

Informal and off-hand technique is the impending direction for cultural meaning. The importance of cultural media and experience native to the language being acquired is foremost in the communicative approach. Musical listening exercises, jigsaw puzzles, warm-up brainstorming templates, idea cluster charts, role-plays, and information-gaps, in both the target language and source language, implement the idea of its culture.

Content Based Approach

Content based teaching, or the use of authentic materials, is encouraged by selecting a subject or topic matter whose interest will extend the students grasp on the target language by allowing their own existent focus to relay itself through it. Descriptive reports on popular media or science are usually supplied.

Total Physical Response Method

In TPR (Total Physical Response) the teacher plays the role of parent and starts by saying a word or a phrase and demonstrating an action. The teacher then says the command and the students all do the action. After repeating a few times it is possible to extend this by asking the students to repeat the word as they do the action. When they feel confident with the word or phrase you can then ask the students to direct each other or the whole class.

It can be used to construct and practice the vocabulary connected with actions; tenses past/present/future and continuous aspects; classroom language; imperatives/Instructions; story-telling.

Discourse Analysis

The Theory of Discourse Analysis penned by Zellig S. Harris in 1952, has developed through its adherence within the linguistic community, as comprehending the cohesive meaning and use of linguistic units, composed in various sentences - such as: arguments, conversations, or speeches.

Pragmatics

Pragmatics, a theory penned by Charles W. Morris focuses on the distinction between speaker meaning and sentence meaning; the former being the literal meaning or sign and the latter the concept the speaker is trying to convey or interpret. It is separated from semantics and syntax; the former, which is the actual ideas or objects a word refers to, and the latter being the form/structure within which something is expressed.

III. EVALUATING INSTRUCTION

Natural Approach

In the Natural Approach, tests are always oral because the goal of this technique is communication. One main guideline of Natural Approach is that there is no direct error correction during communication activities. Students attend to the input; the instructor reacts to the meaning of the message and not the form. By restating the question, restating the response, using the blackboard, the students can hear and see the correct form, but the conversation, dialogue, or communicative activity continues without interrupting work on grammar, pronunciation, or vocabulary items. The instructor can always go back and mention specific items for review at the end of the activity if necessary. There is a low level of anxiety.

The instructor maintains the target language throughout the class by modifying their speech somewhat, using TPR and pictures. Students study rules and practice drills at home. The class time is devoted to introducing enough vocabulary and structure to participate in communicative activities where meaningful language is exchanged. Students work in pairs or small groups. Peer correction is encouraged; students encourage and support each other.

Audio-Lingual Approach

As we have already mentioned, the audio-lingual approach to listening emphasizes first listening to pronunciation and grammatical forms and then imitating those forms by way of drills and exercises. Students are encouraged to listen carefully either to a taped recording of, or a teacher reading out, a dialogue or drill. They then record their own version or respond to cues from the teacher to repeat parts of the dialogue or drill. Basically, the more the students repeat a "correct" phrase/sentence, the stronger their memory of the structure will be. Therefore, students must listen and repeat similar words and sentence structures many times in order to remember them. If a student makes an incorrect response, the teacher corrects the student before continuing with the exercise.

Grammar Approach

A grammar approach to listening usually has students look at a written text while they listen to a recording. This forces them to do several things: identify words by their position in the sentence, work out the relationship between words and phrases, use forward and backward inference cues, and make intelligent guesses based on textual cues. Each listening exercise is more of a test of listening ability than a means of developing specific listening skills. The exercise requires listening for specific vocabulary. There is no attempt to teach lexical meaning or to relate the text to anything other than the task at hand. It is examination oriented.

Communicative Approach

In the communicative method goals and objectives are set through the curriculum and by teacher or student input which are followed through with the selection of activities for the teacher and his students to play out in a controlled setting. The aim is for the student to be placed into an environment where he is patterned into making his own corrections based on the readily available i.e. comprehensible input surrounding him as a living system. The end idea is to achieve socio-linguistic competence as a result of the constant communicative interaction with the student.

Portfolios and projects are the desired end to the communicative focus with the cultural and intra-cultural method of task based learning. Casual conversation is stressed through the hands on influence of the teacher and the constant flow of colloquial cultural maneuvers and events.

Content-Based Approach

In the content based approach (the use of authentic materials) use three or four suitable sources that deal with different aspects of the subject. These could be websites, reference books, audio or video of lectures or even real people. Divide the class into small groups and assign each group a small research task and their source of information to use to help them fulfill the task. Then once they have done their research they form new groups with students that used different information sources and share and compare their information. There should then be some product as the end result of this sharing of information, which could take the form of a group report or presentation of some kind.

Total Physical Response Method

As we have also seen, in TPR (Total Physical Response) the teacher plays the role of parent and starts by saying a word or a phrase and demonstrating an action. The teacher then says the command and the students all do the action. After repeating a few times it is possible to extend this by asking the students to repeat the word as they do the action. When they feel confident with the word or phrase you can then ask the students to direct each other or the whole class.

It can be used to construct and practice the vocabulary connected with actions; tenses past/present/future and continuous aspects; classroom language; imperatives/Instructions; story-telling.

* * *

Selected Bibliography

The American Heritage Spanish Dictionary (1986). Boston: Houghton Mifflin.

Diccionario de la Lengua Española (2003) 23rd ed. Madrid: Real Academia Española

Diccionario Manual VOX Ilustrado de la lengua Española Nueva Edición (1996). Barcelona: Espasa-Calpe

Blair, Rober W. (ed.) (1982). *Innovative Approaches to Language Teaching.* Massachusetts: Newbery House.

Cantarino, Vicente (1986). Civilización y cutura de España (2nd ed.) New Jersey: Prentice Hall.

Chan-Rodríguez, Raquel, and Filer, Malva E. (1988). *Voces de hispanoamérica: antología literaria.* Boston: Heinle & Heinle.

Garcìa, Carme and Spinelli, Emily. (1995). *Mejor dicho.* Massachusetts: D.C. Heath.

Gill, Mary McVey, Wegmann, B., and Mèndez-Faith, T. (1995). *Encontacto: lecturas intermedias* (5th ed.) New York: Harcourt Brace.

Guntermann, Gail (ed.) (1993). *Developing Language Teachers for a Changing World.* Illinois: National Textbook Company.

Hashemipur, Peggy, Maldonado, R., and Van Naerssen, M. (eds.) (1995). Studies in Language Learning and Spanish Linguistics. New York: McGraw-Hill.

Keen, Benjamin (1992). *A History of Latin America* (4th ed). Boston: Houghton Mifflin.

Liskin-Gasparro, Judith (1987. *Testing & Teaching for Oral Proficiency.* Boston: Heinle & Heinle.

Marin, Diego, and del Río, Angel. (1966). *Breve historia de la literatura española.* New York: Holt, Rinehart and Winston.

Marqués, Sarah. (1992). *La lengua que heredamos: curso de español para Bilingües.* (2nd ed.) New York: John Wilery & Sons.

Omaggio Hadley, Alice (1993). *Teaching language in context.* (2nd ed.) Boston: Heinle & Heinle.

Rojas, Jorge Nelson & Curry, Richard A. (1995). *Gramática esencial: repaso y práctica.* Boston: Houghton Mifflin.

Samaniego, Fabián A., Alarcón, F.X., Rojas, N., & Gorman, S.E. (1995). *Mundo 21.* Massachusetts: D.C. Heath.

Spinelli, Emily, Garcia, C., & Galvin, C.E. (1994). *Interacciones.* (2nd ed.). Florida: Holt, Rinehart, and Winston.

*   *   *

REGULAR VERB CONJUGATIONS
MIRAR

Commands: (Imperative) look
Informal: mira tú; no mires
Formal: mire Ud.; miren Uds.

Present Indicative	Preterite Indicative	Imperfect Indicative	Present Progressive	Present Subjunctive
look/looks/looking	*looked*	*looked/used to look*	*am/are/is +*	*look*
do (does) look	*did look*	*was(were) looking*	*looking*	*may look*
miro	miré	miraba	estoy mirando	mire
miras	miraste	mirabas	estás mirando	mires
mira	miró	miraba	está mirando	mire
miramos	miramos	mirábamos	estamos mirando	miremos
miráis	mirasteis	mirabais	estáis mirando	miréis
miran	miraron	miraban	están mirando	miren

Imperfect Subjunctive	Past Progressive	Present Perfect Indicative	Pluperfect Indicative	Future Indicative
looked	*Was/were +*	*have/has*	*had*	*will*
might look	*Looking*	*looked*	*looked*	*look*
mirara	Estaba mirando	he mirado	había mirado	miraré
miraras	estabas mirando	has mirado	habías mirado	mirarás
mirara	Estaba mirando	ha mirado	había mirado	mirará
miráramos	estábamos mirando	hemos mirado	habíamos mirado	miraremos
mirarais	estabais mirando	habéis mirado	habíais mirado	miraréis
miraran	estaban mirando	han mirado	habían mirado	mirarán

Conditional Indicative	Present Perfect Subjunctive	Past Perfect Subjunctive	Future Perfect Indicative	Conditional Perfect Indicative
would	*may have*	*might have*	*will have*	*would have*
look	*looked*	*looked*	*looked*	*looked*
miraría	Haya mirado	hubiera mirado	habré mirado	habría mirado
mirarías	hayas mirado	hubieras mirado	habrás mirado	habrías mirado
miraría	Haya mirado	hubiera mirado	habrá mirado	habría mirado
miraríamos	hayamos mirado	hubiéramos mirado	habremos mirado	habríamos mirado
miraríais	hayáis mirado	hubierais mirado	habréis mirado	habríais mirado
mirarían	hayan mirado	hubieran mirado	habrán mirado	habrían mirado

COMER

Commands: (Imperative) eat
Informal: come tú; no comas
Formal: coma Ud.; coman Uds.

Present Indicative	Preterite Indicative	Imperfect Indicative	Present Progressive	Present Subjunctive
eat/eats/eating	Ate	ate/used to eat	am/are/is	eat
do (does) eat	did eat	was(were) eating	eating	may eat
como	Comí	comía	estoy comiendo	coma
comes	comiste	comías	estás comiendo	comas
come	Comió	comía	está comiendo	coma
comemos*	comimos	comíamos	estamos comiendo	comamos
coméis*	comisteis	comíais	estáis comiendo	comáis
comen	comieron	comían	están comiendo	coman

Imperfect Subjunctive	Past Progressive	Present Perfect Indicative	Pluperfect Indicative	Future Indicative
ate	was/were +	have/has	had	will
might eat	eating	eaten	eaten	eat
comiera	estaba comiendo	he comido	había comido	comeré
comieras	estabas comiendo	has comido	habías comido	comerás
comiera	estaba comiendo	ha comido	había comido	comerá
comiéramos	estábamos comiendo	hemos comido	habíamos comido	comeremos
comierais	estabais comiendo	habéis comido	habíais comido	comeréis
comieran	estaban comiendo	han comido	habían comido	comerán

Conditional Indicative	Present Perfect Subjunctive	Past Perfect Subjunctive	Future Perfect Indicative	Conditional Perfect Indicative
would	may have	might have	will have	would have
eat	Eaten	eaten	eaten	eaten
comería	haya comido	hubiera comido	habré comido	habría comido
comerías	hayas comido	hubieras comido	habrás comido	habrías comido
comería	haya comido	hubiera comido	habrá comido	habría comido
comeríamos	hayamos comido	hubiéramos comido	habremos comido	habríamos comido
comeríais	hayáis comido	hubierais comido	habréis comido	habríais comido
comerían	hayan comido	hubieran comido	habrán comido	habrían comido

*Note: -er and –ir verbs share the same verb endings except for the *nosotros* and *vosotros* forms in the present indicative:
  -er verbs end in *–emos/-éis*   -ir verbs end in *–imos/ -ís*

VIVIR
Commands: (Imperative) live
Informal: vive tú; no vivas
Formal: viva Ud.; vivan Uds.

Present Indicative	Preterite Indicative	Imperfect Indicative	Present Progressive	Present Subjunctive
live/lives/living	*Lived*	*lived/used to live*	*am/are/is*	*live*
do (does) live	*did live*	*was(were) living*	*living*	*may live*
vivo	Viví	vivía	estoy viviendo	viva
vives	viviste	vivías	estás viviendo	vivas
vive	Vivió	vivía	está viviendo	viva
vivimos	vivimos	vivíamos	estamos viviendo	vivamos
vivís	vivisteis	vivíais	estáis viviendo	viváis
viven	vivieron	vivían	están viviendo	vivan

Imperfect Subjunctive	Past Progressive	Present Perfect Indicative	Pluperfect Indicative	Future Indicative
lived	*was/were +*	*have/has*	*had*	*will*
might live	*living*	*lived*	*lived*	*live*
viviera	estaba viviendo	he vivido	había vivido	viviré
vivieras	estabas viviendo	has vivido	habías vivido	vivirás
viviera	estaba viviendo	ha vivido vivido	había vivido	vivirá
viviéramos	estábamos viviendo	hemos vivido	habíamos vivido	viviremos
vivierais	Estabais viviendo	habéis vivido	habíais vivido	viviréis
vivieran	estaban viviendo	han vivido	habían vivido	vivirán

TEACHER CERTIFICATION STUDY GUIDE

Conditional Indicative	Present Perfect Subjunctive	Past Perfect Subjunctive	Future Perfect Indicative	Conditional Perfect Indicative
would *live*	*may have* *lived*	*might have* *lived*	*will have* *lived*	*would have* *lived*
viviría	haya vivido	hubiera vivido	habré vivido	habría vivido
vivirías	Hayas vivido	hubieras vivido	habrás vivido	habrías vivido
viviría	haya vivido	hubiera vivido	habrá vivido	habría vivido
viviríamos	hayamos vivido	hubiéramos vivido	habremos vivido	habríamos vivido
viviríais	Hayáis vivido	hubiera vivido	habréis vivido	habríais vivido
vivirían	Hayan vivido	hubieran vivido	habrán vivido	habrían vivido

Comon Verbs with Irregular Forms in the Present Subjunctive

The present subjunctive is formed by first conjugating the infinitive in the first person in the present indicative. Always begin with the infinitive.

Examples:

Infinitive	First Person	Indicative	Subjunctive
mirar	yo	miro	mire
comer	yo	como	coma
vivir	yo	vivo	viva
decir	yo	digo	diga
hacer	yo	hago	haga

Infinitivo	First Person	Indicative	Subjunctive
poner	yo	pongo	ponga
pensar	yo	pienso	piense
contar	yo	cuento	cuente
servir	yo	sirvo	sirva
morir	yo	muero	muera

Exceptions are the six Spanish verbs that do not end in –o in the first person singular:

Infinitive	First person	Indicative	Subjunctive
Dar	yo	doy	dé
Estar	yo	estoy	esté
Ser	yo	soy	sea
Ir	yo	voy	vaya
Saber	yo	sé	sepa
Haber	yo	he	haya

Common Verbs with Irregular Forms in the First Person Singular

Present Indicative

Infinitive	yo	tú	él/ella/Ud.	nosotros/as	vosotros/as	ellos/ellas/Uds.
Caber	quepo	cabes	cabe	cabemos	cabéis	caben
Conocer	conozco	conoces	conoce	conocemos	conocéis	conocen
Dar	doy	das	da	damos	dais	dan
Hacer	hago	haces	hace	hacemos	hacéis	hacen
Poner	pongo	pones	pone	ponemos	ponéis	ponen
Saber	sé	sabes	sabe	sabemos	sabéis	saben
Salir	salgo	sales	sale	salimos	salís	salen
Traer	traigo	traes	trae	traemos	traéis	traen
Valer	valgo	vales	vale	valemos	valéis	valen
Ver	veo	ves	ve	vemos	veis	ven

Common Verbs with Irregular Forms in the Future and Conditional Indicative

The future and conditional tenses are formed by adding a series of endings to the entire infinitive or to a corrupted infinitive. The endings work for all verbs, no exceptions: -ar, -er, -ir.

Note the forms of the Present Perfect of haber	Future Endings	Infinitive	Corrupted Infinitive	Conditional Endings
He	-é	haber	habr-	-ía
Has	-ás	poder	podr-	-ías
Ha	-á	querer	querr-	-ía
Hemos	-emos	saber	sabr-	-íamos
		venir	vendr-	
		poner	pondr-	
		salir	saldr-	
		tener	tendr-	
		valer	valdr-	
		decir	dir-	
		hacer	har-	

Common Verbs with Irregular Forms in the Preterite Indicative

Meaning	Infinitive	yo	tú	él/ella/ud.	nosotros/as	vosotros/as	ellos/ellas/uds.
to have	tener	tuve	tuviste	tuvo	tuvimos	tuvisteis	tuvieron
to be	estar	estuve	estuviste	estuvo	estuvimos	estuvisteis	estuvieron
to walk	andar	anduve	anduviste	anduvo	anduvimos	anduvisteis	anduvieron
to know	saber	supe	supiste	supo	supimos	supisteis	supieron
to put	poner	puse	pusiste	puso	pusimos	pusisteis	pusieron
to be able	poder	pude	pudiste	pudo	pudimos	pudisteis	pudieron
to want	querer	quise	quisiste	quiso	quisimos	quisteis	quisieron
to do, make	hacer	hice	hiciste	hizo	hicimos	hicisteis	hicieron
to come	venir	vine	viniste	vino	vinimos	vinisteis	vinieron
to say, tell	decir	dije	dijiste	dijo	dijimos	dijisteis	dijeron
to bring	traer	traje	trajiste	trajo	trajimos	trajisteis	trajeron
to give	dar	di	diste	dio	dimos	disteis	dieron
to see	ver	vi	viste	vio	vimos	visteis	vieron
to go	ir	fui	fuiste	fue	fuimos	fuisteis	fueron
to be	ser	fui	fuiste	fue	fuimos	fuisteis	fueron

Verbs Irregular in the Imperfect

There are only three irregular verbs in the Imperfect tense.

Meaning	Infinitive	yo	tú	él/ella/Ud.	nosotros/as	vosotros/as	ellos/ellas/Uds.
to be	ser	Era	eras	era	éramos	erais	eran
to go	ir	Iba	ibas	iba	íbamos	ibais	iban
to see	ver	Veía	veías	veía	veíamos	veíais	veían

Regular and Irregular Past Participles

To form the past participle, simply drop the infinitive ending (-ar, -er, -ir) and add -ado (for -ar verbs) or -ido (for -er, -ir verbs).

hablar - ar + ado = hablado

comer - er + ido = comido

vivir - ir + ido = vivido

The following common verbs have irregular past participles:

abrir	-	abierto
cubrir	-	cubierto
decir	-	dicho
escribir	-	escrito
freír	-	frito
hacer	-	hecho
morir	-	muerto
poner	-	puesto
resolver	-	resuelto
romper	-	roto
ver	-	visto
volver	-	vuelto

Note that compound verbs based on the irregular verbs inherit the same irregularities. Here are a few examples:

> componer - compuesto
>
> describir - descrito
>
> devolver - devuelto

Most past participles can be used as adjectives. Like other adjectives, they agree in gender and number with the nouns that they modify.

> La tienda está <u>cerrada</u>.
>
> Las tiendas están <u>cerradas</u>.
>
> El cajón está <u>abierto</u>.
>
> Los cajones están <u>abiertos</u>.

The past participle can be combined with the verb "ser" to express the passive voice. Use this construction when an action is being described, and introduce the doer of the action with the word "por."

> La casa fue <u>construida</u> por los albañiles.
>
> El cristal de la ventana fue roto por los niños al jugar.

Note that for -er and -ir verbs, if the stem ends in a vowel, a written accent will be required.

> creer - creído
>
> oír - oído

Note: this rule does not apply, and no written accent is required for verbs ending in -uir. (construir, seguir, influir, distinguir, etc.)

MAP OF SPAIN

Library of Congress, Geography and Map Division. Call # G6560 1982.U5

TEACHER CERTIFICATION STUDY GUIDE

MAP OF LATIN AMERICA

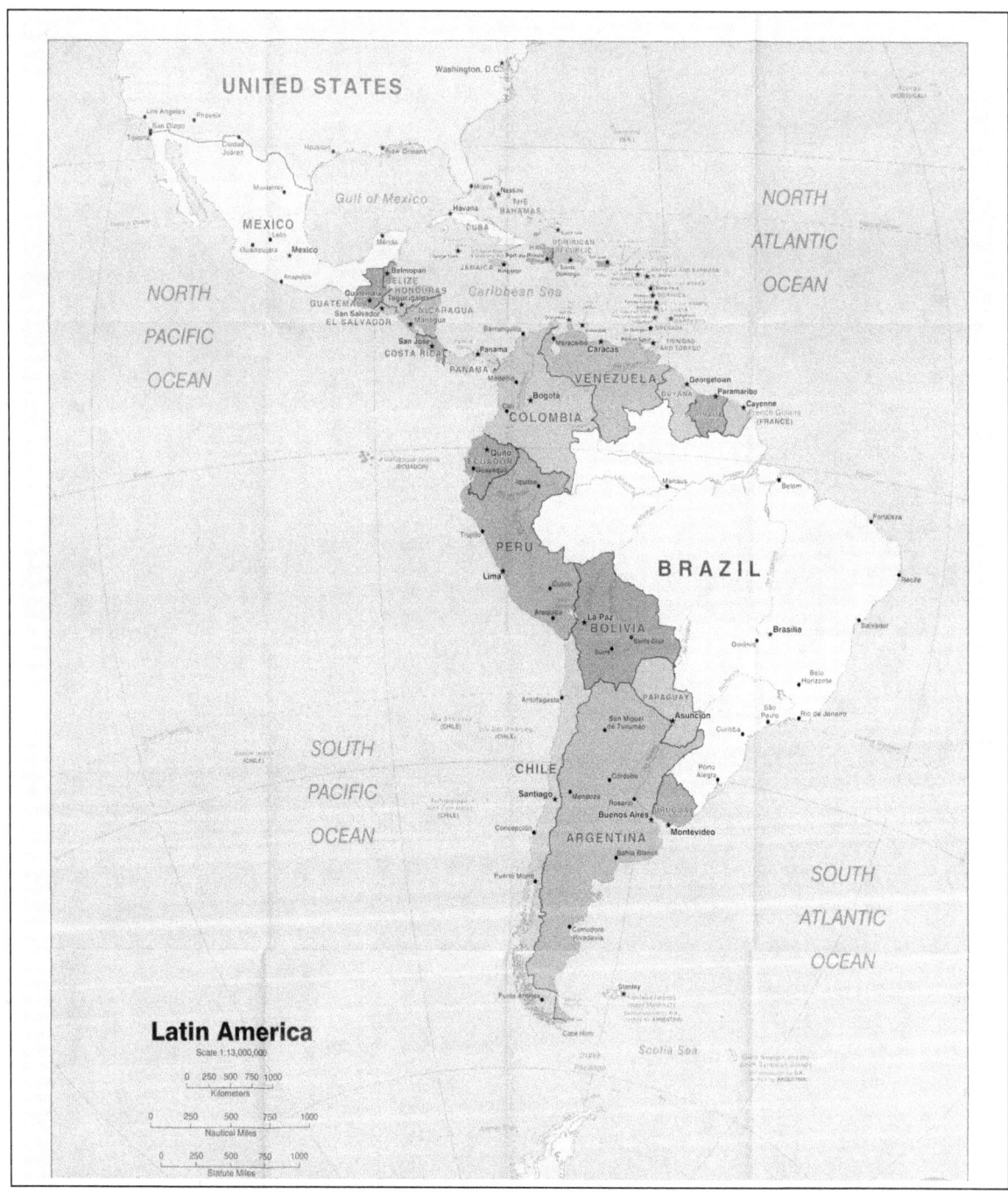

Library of Congress, Geography and Map Division. Call # G3292.L3 2006.U5

MAP OF THE CARIBBEAN

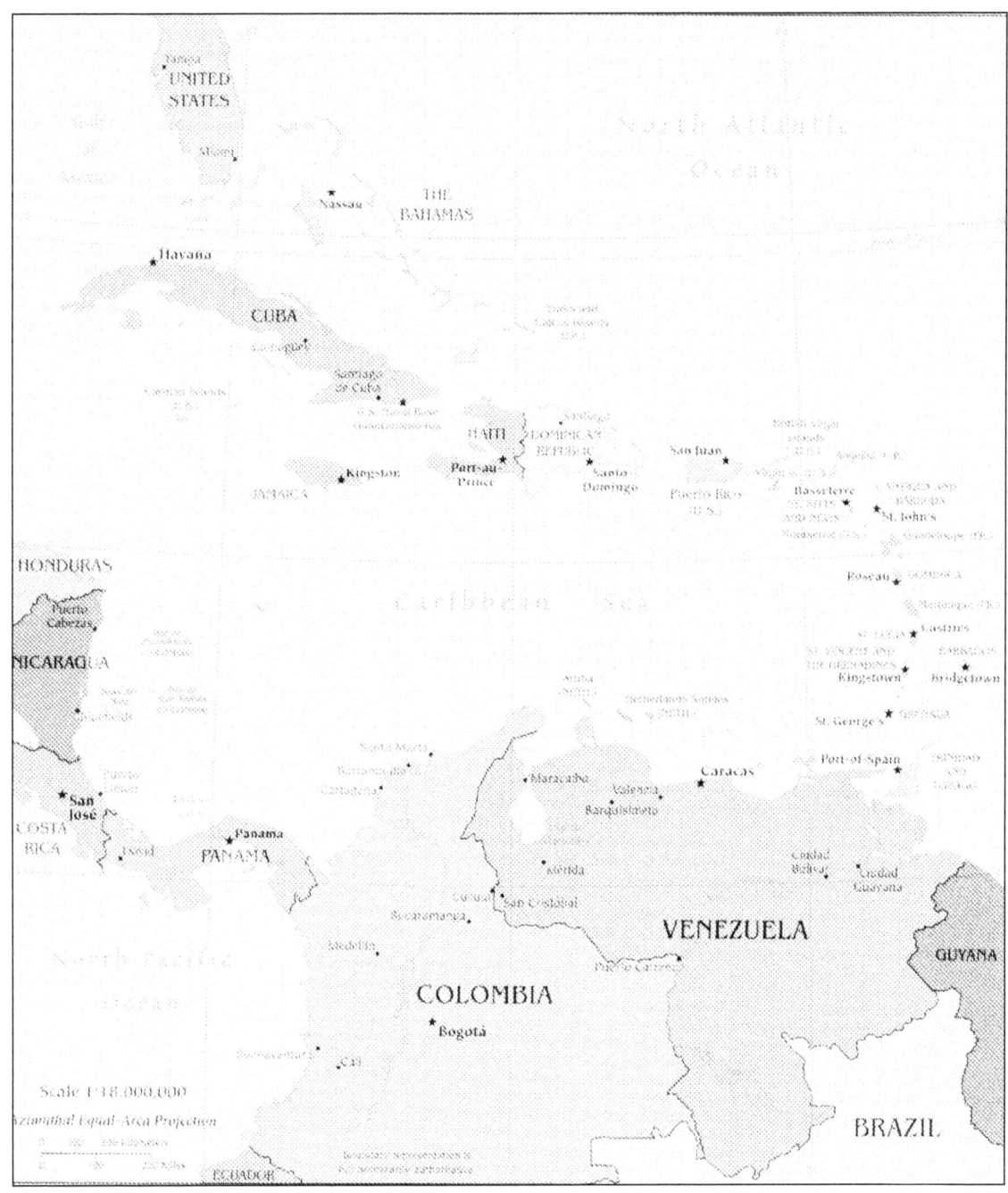

Library of Congress, Geography and Map Division. Call # G4390 2006.U49

SAMPLE TEST

Directions: Read each item and select the best response.

SPEAKING SECTION

For this section of the state exam you will be asked to record your answers in Spanish. Follow all directions on the cassette tape provided at the exam site.

Give the following directions in Spanish:

1. Take out your books.
   (Easy)

2. Pick up your papers and books.
   (Easy)

3. Write your answers on the blackboard.
   (Easy)

4. Please, get into groups of four or five.
   (Rigorous)

5. Complete the following for homework.
   (Average Rigor)

6. Hand in your homework.
   (Easy)

7. Describe where you went on your last vacation and what you did there.
   (Average Rigor)

8. Explain what sporting event(s) you plan to watch or attend this coming season: with whom, where, and why?
   (Rigorous)

9. Narrate and explain how you spent your last major holiday.
   (Average Rigor)

10. Describe how you will spend your next family celebration.
    (Average Rigor)

11. María, explain what your favorite book is and why.
    (Easy)

12. Paolo, describe your favorite kind of music.
    (Easy)

13. Dave, what hobby would you like to pursue in more depth?
    (Rigorous)

14. Lisa, explain a news story you have been following in the paper or on the television.
    (Average Rigor)

15. Chad, describe a political event or story of importance to you.
    (Average Rigor)

16. Consuelo, where do you live and why do you live there?
    (Easy)

17. Latasha, what advice would you like to give to the president about the importance of education funding in the 21st century?
    (Rigorous)

18. Ben, what do you think about efforts being done to save the environment in your state and in the country in general? Why?
    (Rigorous)

19. Manuel, what would you advise students about working long hours after school? Defend your opinion.
    (Rigorous)

20. Kate, do you think professional athletes should be held to higher standards than other public figures? Why?
    (Rigorous)

LISTENING SECTION www.xamonline.com

Please note a written script is provided in these sample materials. However, the state examination will not include a written text, written questions, or written choices. **For the actual audio file, visit our website at www.xamonline.com**

Listen carefully to the following passages and questions. Answer the following based upon what you heard. (*Audio script is in italics*)

21. ¿Cuál es el propósito del viaje de Rigoberto Menchú a España?
    (Easy)

    Rigoberta Menchú, una indígena Guatemalteca que nació en 1959, ganó el Premio Nóbel de la Paz en 1992. Viajará a varios países, entre ellos, España. Menchú va a estar en Madrid donde dialogará con el nuevo presidente del gobierno español. Menchú va a discutir las maneras en que sufre la población indígena de América Latina. Rigoberta Menchú ha dedicado sus esfuerzos y trabajo de vida a este grupo.

    ¿Cuál es el propósito del viaje de Rigoberto Menchú a España?

    A. Viajar a varios países europeos

    B. Conocer personalmente al Príncipe Felipe de Borbón

    C. Recibir el Premio Nóbel de la Paz

    D. Hablar sobre sus esfuerzos por las comunidades indígenas

22. **¿Qué se destaca en este texto que le gusta al Príncipe Felipe?** *(Average Rigor)*

El Príncipe Felipe de Borbón, el futuro líder de España, nació en 1968. Estudió en Canadá y en Estados Unidos. Es muy atlético y le interesan mucho los deportes. Aunque el príncipe es famoso lleva una vida bastante normal. Está bien preparado para ser el próximo Rey de España, según los políticos europeos.

¿Qué se destaca en este texto que le gusta al Príncipe Felipe?

A. Conversar con los norteamericanos

B. Visitar las universidades canadienses

C. Practicar deportes

D. Visitar ciudades norteamericanas

23. **¿Cómo cambió mi estilo de vida?** *(Average Rigor)*

Antes de obtener mi licencia de conducir, yo siempre tenía que depender de otras personas para salir de paseo. No era independiente. No podía salir con mis amigos impulsivamente. Ahora tengo más libertad e independencia.

¿Cómo cambió mi estilo de vida?

A. Radicalmente

B. Impulsivamente

C. Solamente

D. Dependiente

24. ¿Adónde van ellos primero?
    (Easy)

    Por favor, mañana tienes que salir temprano conmigo para ir de compras, porque voy a tener una fiesta el sábado. Espero que haya tortillas en la Bodega García, porque no tengo tiempo para ir al supermercado Solano, lejos en Miami. ¡Ojalá que yo tenga suficiente comida para todos los invitados!

    ¿Adónde van ellos primero?

    A. Una fiesta

    B. Al supermercado

    C. A una bodega

    D. A Miami

25. ¿Qué deben comprar?
    (Rigorous)

    En la sala sólo hay un sillón de cuero y una lámpara; entonces necesitamos un sofá para sentarnos y una televisión para ver nuestros programas favoritos. En el comedor nos falta una mesa grande; aunque hay seis sillas.

    ¿Qué deben comprar?

    A. Un sillón de cuero y una lámpara

    B. Un sofá, una televisión y una mesa grande

    C. Una mesa grande y seis sillas

    D. No nos falta nada

STRUCTURE OF THE LANGUAGE
Choose the best written item.

26. *(Average Rigor)*

    A. Es necesario que él estudiar.

    B. Es necesario que él estudié.

    C. Es necesario que él estudie.

    D. Es necesario que él estudia.

27. *(Easy)*

    A. Necesito leer el libro.

    B. Necesito que yo leo el libro.

    C. Necesito que yo lea el libro.

    D. Necesito que yo leer el libro.

28. *(Easy)*

    A. El lápiz de el es azul.

    B. Él lápiz de el es azul.

    C. El lápiz de él es azul.

    D. Él lápiz de él es azul.

29. *(Rigorous)*

    A. Si tuviera el dinero viajara a Japón.

    B. Si tuviera el dinero viajará a Japón.

    C. Si tuviera el dinero viajaré a Japón.

    D. Si tuviera el dinero viajaría a Japón.

30. *(Rigorous)*

    A. ¡Que pena que él se fuera!

    B. ¡Qué pena que él se fue!

    C. ¡Que pena qué él se fue!

    D. ¡Qué pena que él se fuera!

31. *(Easy)*

    A. ¿Porque lo hiciste tú?

    B. ¿Por qué lo hiciste tú?

    C. ¿Por qué lo hiciste tu?

    D. ¿Porque lo hiciste tu?

32. *(Rigorous)*

    A. Se prohibe fumar.

    B. El fumar es prohibido.

    C. La fumar es prohibido.

    D. Fumando es prohibido.

33. *(Average Rigor)*

    A. Además de leer, me gusta nadando.

    B. Además de leyendo, me gusta nadando.

    C. Además de leer, me gusta nadar.

    D. Además de leyendo, me gusta nadar.

34. *(Average Rigor)*

    A. Nos gusta esquiar y navegar.

    B. Nos gustamos esquiar y navegar.

    C. Nos gusta esquiando y navegando.

    D. Nos gusta esquiar e navegar.

35. *(Rigorous)*

    A. Se me olvidé la cartera.

    B. Se me olvidó la cartera.

    C. Me la olvidó la cartera.

    D. Me la olvidé la cartera.

36. *(Rigorous)*

    A. Cuando regresamos de México vamos mostrarle las fotos.

    B. Cuando regresemos de México vamos a mostrarle los fotos.

    C. Cuando regresemos de México vamos a mostrarle las fotos.

    D. Cuando regresamos de México vamos a mostrarle los fotos.

37. *(Easy)*

    A. Los regalos son para tú.

    B. Los regalos son para tu.

    C. Los regalos son para ti.

    D. Los regalos son para te.

38. *(Rigorous)*

   A. En mí opinión, la gente es muy buena.

   B. En mi opinión, la gente es muy buena.

   C. En mi opinión, la gente son muy buena.

   D. En mí opinión, la gente son muy buena.

39. *(Average Rigor)*

   A. ¿Viste a Mónica y a Carmen?

   B. ¿Viste Mónica a Carmen?

   C. ¿Viste a Mónica Carmen?

   D. ¿Viste Mónica y Carmen?

40. *(Rigorous)*

   A. Se puso la chaqueta por el frío.

   B. Se puso la chaqueta como el frío.

   C. Puso la chaqueta por el frío.

   D. Puso la chaqueta para el frío.

Choose the correct response or most appropriate rejoinder:

41. ¿Quién lo hizo?
    (Average Rigor)

    A. —Yo lo hice.

    B. —Yo me hice.

    C. —Yo lo hizo.

    D. —Me lo hizo.

42. ¿Cuándo estudiaste para el examen?
    (Easy)

    A. —Estudió anoche por dos horas.

    B. —Estudio anoche por dos horas.

    C. —Estudiaste anoche por dos horas.

    D. —Estudié anoche por dos horas.

43. Él habla tres idiomas.
    (Easy)

    A. —¡Qué bien que habla tres idiomas!

    B. —¡Qué bien que hable tres idiomas!

    C. —¡Que bien que hablo tres idiomas!

    D. —¡Que bien que hablas tres idiomas!

44. Me dolía la cabeza la semana pasada.
    (Rigorous)

    A. —¿Fue al médico?

    B. —¿Fue el médico?

    C. —¿Iba el médico?

    D. —¿Fuiste el médico?

45. ¿Lo conociste en el colegio?
    (Rigorous)

    A. —Sí, lo conoció allí.

    B. —Sí, me conocí allí.

    C. —Sí, lo conocí allí.

    D. —Sí, me lo conoció allí.

46. Nosotras hemos_____una novela.
    (Average Rigor)

    A. escrito

    B. escribido

    C. escribida

    D. escrita

47. Mi tía ha _____ muy joven.
    (Rigorous)

    A. morido

    B. muerta

    C. muerto

    D. morida

48. ¿Cuándo prepararás la comida?
    (Easy)

    A. –La preparé mañana.

    B. –La prepararás mañana.

    C. –La prepara mañana.

    D. –La prepararé mañana.

49. Change the following sentence to passive voice: "María compró la pintura de Dalí."
    (Rigorous)

    A. La pintura de Dalí es comprada por María.

    B. La pintura de Dalí se compra por María.

    C. La pintura de Dalí fue comprada por María.

    D. La pintura de Dalí se compró por María.

50. *(Average Rigor)*

    A. –¿Mira Ud. al espejo cuando peinarse?

    B. –¿Se mira Ud. al espejo cuando peina?

    C. –¿Ud. mirase al espejo cuando peina?

    D. –¿Se mira Ud. al espejo cuando se peina?

51. *(Average Rigor)*

    A. Mis clases son bastantes difíciles, pero tengo mucha gente que me ayuda.

    B. Mis clases son bastante difíciles, pero tengo mucha gente que me ayuda.

    C. Mis clases son bastante difícil, pero tengo mucha gente que me ayuda.

    D. Mis clases son bastantes difíciles, pero tengo mucho gente que me ayuda.

52. Tenemos problemas políticos y sociales. Necesitamos mejorar_____.
    (Rigorous)

    A. politicamente y socialmente

    B. políticamente y socialmente

    C. política y socialmente

    D. política y socialmente

53. *(Easy)*

    A. Esto lo hizo Juan o Oscar.

    B. Esto lo hizo Juan e Oscar.

    C. Miguel e Inés juegan al balón.

    D. Miguel y Inés juegan al balón.

54. *(Easy)*

    A. Habla del niño.

    B. Habla a el niño.

    C. Habla de el niño.

    D. Habla en el niño.

55. Si un español dice: "Me gusta comer palomitas en mi coche", un argentino diría:
    (Rigorous)

    A. Me gusta comer pochochos en mi coche.

    B. Me gusta comer pochoclos en mi auto.

    C. Me gusta comer porotos en mi carro.

    D. Me gusta comer cabritas en mi carro.

56. **Choose the correct written form for the numerical expression "551 bombillas."**
    (Average Rigor)

    A. Quinientos, cincuenta y uno

    B. Quinientas cincuentaiuno

    C. Quinientas y cincuenta y una

    D. Quinientas cincuenta y una

57. Choose the correct written form of the date.
    (Easy)

    A. 14 de Febrero, 1999

    B. 14 de febrero de 1999

    C. Febrero, 14 de 1999

    D. 14, febrero de 1999

58. Choose the correct idiomatic expression.
    (Average Rigor)

    Miguel saludó a Rosa en la escalera, pero ella no se dio cuenta porque es muy despistada;...

    A. siempre anda en los sueños.

    B. siempre anda en la luna.

    C. siempre está en el aire.

    D. siempre está en Marte.

59. Choose the correct idiomatic expression.
    (Average Rigor)

    Pedro quería decirnos algo, pero daba tantos detalles que al final le dije:...

    A. –¡Basta, ve al grano!

    B. –¡Basta, ve al centro!

    C. –¡Basta, ve al núcleo!

    D. –¡Basta, ve al punto!

60. Hay 6 chicas en la clase. Juana tiene 1.80 m. de altura. Todas las otras chicas tienen menos. Juana es _____ la clase.
    (Rigorous)

    A. la menos alta de

    B. más alta que

    C. la más alta que

    D. la más alta de

61. Luis tiene muchas fotos. Enrique tiene muchas fotos también.
    (Rigorous)

    A. Luis tiene menos fotos que Enrique.

    B. Enrique tiene tantas fotos como Luis.

    C. Enrique tiene más fotos que Luis.

    D. Enrique tiene tantas fotos que Luis.

62. **Me importan los asuntos de lo que habíamos hablado.**
    (Average Rigor)

    A. –A mi me importan tampoco.

    B. –A mí me importan también.

    C. –A mi me importan tambien.

    D. –A mí me importan tampoco.

Choose the rule or explanation that best explains the following:

63. **Esta mañana Lisette tomaba el sol y yo me bañaba en el mar.** *(Rigorous)*

    A. Incorrect: The two verbs should be in the preterite because the actions occurred at a specific time.

    B. Incorrect: The subordinate verb should be in the preterite tense to contrast the two main events.

    C. Incorrect: The use of "bañarse" is not appropriate.

    D. Correct: The imperfect tense can be used to describe two or more actions going on at the same time in the past.

64. **Eran las 2:00 cuando salimos ayer por la tarde.** *(Rigorous)*

    A. Correct: The imperfect tense is used to tell time in the past.

    B. Incorrect: Both verbs should be in the imperfect to describe past actions.

    C. Incorrect: The preterite tense is used to tell time in the past.

    D. Correct: Both verbs are in the imperfect tense to tell a story.

65. **Trabajamos para dos horas.** *(Average Rigor)*

    A. Correct: "Para" is used to indicate a deadline.

    B. Correct: "Para" is used to indicate a length of time.

    C. Incorrect: "Por" is used to indicate a specific hour.

    D. Incorrect: "Por" is used to indicate a length of time.

66. **Si hubiera más casas baratas, podría comprar una en vez de alquilar.** *(Rigorous)*

   A. Correct: This is the correct form of the pluperfect and imperfect subjunctive.

   B. Incorrect: The subjunctive and conditional forms cannot be combined in a sentence.

   C. Correct: The "si" clause using the imperfect subjunctive can be used with the conditional in the following clause.

   D. Incorrect: "Hubiera" needs a past participle.

67. **Estaban viendo la televisión cuando alguien cerró la puerta.** *(Rigorous)*

   A. Incorrect: The imperfect tense is used to tell a story.

   B. Incorrect: The imperfect tense is used to indicate past actions.

   C. Correct: The imperfect tense is used to describe the past.

   D. Correct: The imperfect tense sets the stage for another action to take place.

68. **Quisiera que ella lo hiciera.** *(Rigorous)*

   A. Correct: The imperfect subjunctive is used following the preterite.

   B. Correct: The imperfect subjunctive is used following a past subjunctive.

   C. Incorrect: The imperfect subjunctive is used to express doubt in the past.

   D. Correct: The imperfect subjunctive is used to express emotion in the past.

69. **Música es el idioma universal.**
    (Average Rigor)

    A. Incorrect: The definite article is needed with nouns to point out a specific person or thing and is used with nouns expressing an abstract or generalized concept.

    B. Incorrect: The word "idioma" is feminine.

    C. Correct: The word "música" is too general a concept to be labeled "la música."

    D. Correct: The verb "ser" is used to define.

70. **Señora Cabrices es de Caracas, Venezuela.**
    (Average Rigor)

    A. Correct: The verb "ser" is used to express origin or nationality.

    B. Correct: The preposition "a" is not needed.

    C. Incorrect: The verb "estar" is used to express location.

    D. Incorrect: The definite article should precede the title of someone's name.

71. **Mis hermanos y yo somos altas.**
    (Easy)

    A. Correct: The verb "ser" is used to describe physical attributes.

    B. Correct: The compound subject requires the verb "somos."

    C. Correct: The possessive pronoun should be in the plural form.

    D. Incorrect: The plural adjective should be in the masculine plural form.

72. **¿Quién es? ¿Será la niñera?**
    (Rigorous)

    A. Incorrect: The future tense is not used to respond to a question in the present.

    B. Correct: The future tense is used to indicate probability.

    C. Correct: The subject is understood.

    D. Incorrect: The subject should precede the verb.

73. **La problema principal es que no han hecho nada.**
    (Average Rigor)

    A. Correct: Most nouns ending in "–ma" are feminine.

    B. Incorrect: Most nouns ending in "–ma" are masculine.

    C. Correct: The word "no" precedes the present perfect construction.

    D. Correct: Spanish requires the double negative.

74. **Mi padre es pesimista pero mi madre es optimista.**
    (Average Rigor)

    A. Incorrect: Adjectives agree in gender and number with the noun they modify.

    B. Incorrect: The conjunction "sino" should be used in the negative construction.

    C. Correct: Subjunctive mood is not needed to express an opinion.

    D. Correct: Adjectives that end in "–ista" have only one singular form for masculine and feminine nouns.

75. **Si irás conmigo, será mejor.**
    (Rigorous)

    A. Incorrect: The future tense is never used in the "si" clause.

    B. Correct: The future tense is always used in the "si" clause.

    C. Correct: The future tense is used to express probability.

    D. Correct: The "si" clause denotes more of a probability than a possibility.

76. **¿Saben ustedes cómo tocar el piano?**
    (Average Rigor)

    A. Incorrect: "Como" used in a question requires a written accent mark.

    B. Incorrect: "Saber" indicates the knowledge of a fact.

    C. Incorrect: "Saber" to indicate knowledge of how to do something does not require the "cómo."

    D. Correct: "Tocar" means to play a musical instrument and "jugar" means to play a sport or game.

77. **Quiero que él lo haga.**
    (Average Rigor)

    A. Correct: Object pronouns are attached to affirmative direct commands.

    B. Correct: Object pronouns precede a conjugated verb in both the indicative and subjunctive moods.

    C. Incorrect: The present subjunctive is formed by dropping the "–o" of the first person singular of the present indicative.

    D. Incorrect: The subjunctive expresses an implied command.

78. **Se venden muchos autos aquí.**
    (Average Rigor)

    A. Correct: "Se" expresses an unknown plural subject "they."

    B. Correct: The verb is plural to agree with the plural object.

    C. Incorrect: "Se" denotes a reflexive action.

    D. Incorrect: "Se" is only used with the third person singular form of the verb, not the plural.

79. **¡Tú, dime la verdad!**
    (Average Rigor)

    A. Correct: "Tú" as a subject pronoun requires an accent mark.

    B. Correct: "Dar" is an irregular verb when conjugated in the "tú" command form.

    C. Incorrect: The direct and indirect object pronouns should both be attached to the end of the verb "di".

    D. Incorrect: The direct object pronoun should precede the verb."

80. **No lo han leído.**
    (Average Rigor)

    A. Incorrect: The object pronoun precedes the past participle.

    B. Incorrect: The past participle should be plural to agree in number with the subject.

    C. Incorrect: The past participle does not require a written accent mark.

    D. Correct: The object pronoun precedes the entire verb phase.

81. ¿Qué es esto?
    (Average Rigor)

    A. Correct: "Esto" as a neuter demonstrative pronoun does not take a written accent.

    B. Correct: Demonstrative adjectives that replace a noun are called demonstrative pronouns.

    C. Incorrect: "Esto" requires a written accent mark.

    D. Incorrect: Demonstrative pronouns point out.

82. **Vendimos nuestra antigua casa hace muchos años.**
    (Average Rigor)

    A. Incorrect: Only quantitative adjectives precede a noun.

    B. Incorrect: Only qualitative adjectives precede a noun.

    C. Correct: In this context "antigua" denotes the former home.

    D. Correct: In this context "antigua" denotes the very, very, old home.

83. **Estábamos yendo al museo de la Reina Sofía a las dos.**
    (Rigorous)

    A. Incorrect: The present indicative would be more appropriate than the imperfect.

    B. Incorrect: The correct present participle for "ir" is "iendo".

    C. Incorrect: The verb "ir" should be in the preterite *nosotros* form "Fuimos".

    D. Correct: "a" + "el" form the contraction "al" before "museo".

84. **Raúl se comió el pollo.**
    (Average Rigor)

    A. Incorrect: The object should precede the subject of the sentence.

    B. Correct: The verb agrees with the subject of the sentence.

    C. Incorrect: The verb "comer" is not reflexive.

    D. Correct: The verb is in the singular to agree with the object of the sentence.

85. Él es un buen estudiante.
    (Easy)

    A. Incorrect: The qualitative adjective should not precede the noun.

    B. Correct: The verb "estar" implies a temporary quality or condition.

    C. Incorrect: The indefinite article is not used with occupations.

    D. Correct: The adjective "bueno" is shortened before a singular masculine noun.

86. Se me perdieron los libros.
    (Rigorous)

    A. Correct: The "me" is used here as an indirect object pronoun.

    B. Incorrect: The verb should agree in number with the subject of the sentence.

    C. Correct: The "me" is used here as a reflexive pronoun.

    D. Incorrect: The word "se" is not needed with the verb "perder."

87. Anoche estuve enfermo.
    (Average Rigor)

    A. Incorrect: The preterite describes a specific action or event in the past.

    B. Correct: The imperfect describes an emotional activity in the past.

    C. Correct: The preterite can be used to emphasize that an action has ended.

    D. Incorrect: The imperfect expresses a temporary condition in the past.

88. Ayer iba al cine cuando vino Diego.
    (Rigorous)

    A. Correct: The imperfect describes a past repetitive action.

    B. Correct: The imperfect stresses an action in progress when another action took place.

    C. Incorrect: The preterite is needed to express past facts.

    D. Incorrect: The preterite expresses an action that took place at a definite time in the past.

89. **Ella es mayor que yo.**
    (Average Rigor)

    A. Correct: It implies she is physically bigger than I am.

    B. Correct: It implies she is older than I am.

    C. Incorrect: It implies she is the oldest of all.

    D. Incorrect: It implies she is greater than I am.

90. **Hay más que veinte personas.**
    (Rigorous)

    A. Correct: The comparative requires a written accent.

    B. Incorrect: When this comparison is followed by a number, the form is "más de."

    C. Correct: The numeral 20 requires "más de" but not the written form of the number.

    D. Incorrect: The correct comparative is "mayor" for greater than.

91. **Por favor, René, el carro está sucio. Lávalo.**
    (Rigorous)

    A. Incorrect: The command form is not needed here. It is a request.

    B. Incorrect: The object pronoun should precede the conjugated verb.

    C. Correct: The affirmative command is in the familiar form.

    D. Correct: The negative familiar command has the same form as the second person singular.

92. **Isabel me conocía por la primera vez en 1992.**
    (Easy)

    A. Correct: The verb "conocer" denotes knowing a person.

    B. Correct: The verb "saber" denotes factual knowledge.

    C. Correct: The imperfect of "conocer" implies met for the first time.

    D. Incorrect: The preterite of "conocer" implies met for the first time.

93. **El agua es pura.**
    (Average Rigor)

    A. Correct: The word "agua" is masculine.

    B. Correct: "El" is used although the word "agua" is feminine.

    C. Incorrect: The word "agua" is not masculine.

    D. Incorrect: The word "agua" is feminine and it should be "La."

94. **A mí me gusta el chocolate, el vino y el cafe.**
    (Average Rigor)

    A. Correct: Words with natural emphasis on the second to last syllable do not require accent marks.

    B. Incorrect: Accents are required over the second to last syllable of "vino" and the last syllable of "café."

    C. Incorrect: An accent is required on the last syllable of "café."

    D. Incorrect: Both words need accents on their last syllables.

95. **Necesito el informe para el lunes.**
    (Rigorous)

    A. Incorrect: "para" is used to express a length of time.

    B. Correct: "por" is used to express a length of time or specific hour.

    C. Incorrect: "por" is used to indicate a specific deadline.

    D. Correct: "para" is used to indicate a specific deadline.

96. **¿Qué es la capital de Colombia?**
    (Average Rigor)

    A. Correct: "Qué" is used to ask for a definition.

    B. Correct: "Qué" is used to elicit a choice between two or more items.

    C. Correct: "Qué" is used to elicit a choice.

    D. Incorrect: "Cuál" is used to imply a choice in the response.

97. **Los médicos trabajan para el hospital.**
    (Rigorous)

    A. Correct: "para" is used to indicate employed by.

    B. Incorrect: "para" is used to designate the recipient of an action or destination.

    C. Incorrect: "por" is used to indicate employed by.

    D. Incorrect: "por" is used to express occupation.

98. **¿Quieres ir al cine conmigo? No quiero ir contigo.**
    (Average Rigor)

    A. Incorrect: Spanish often requires a multiple, or double, negative construction.

    B. Incorrect: The subjunctive is used to express a wish, desire or emotion.

    C. Correct: "No" precedes the verb.

    D. Incorrect: The direct object can be used at the end of an infinitive.

TEACHER CERTIFICATION STUDY GUIDE

CULTURAL PERSPECTIVES

Choose the appropriate answer to complete the following items.

99. **José Martí (1853-1895), era de ___.**
    (Average Rigor)

    A. México

    B. Chile

    C. Cuba

    D. Argentina

100. **En 1971, Pablo Neruda (1904-1973) recibió el Premio Nóbel de ___.**
    (Average Rigor)

    A. Literatura

    B. Arte

    C. Ciencia

    D. la Paz

101. **Machu Picchu, en el Perú, es la antigua ciudad sagrada de los ___.**
    (Easy)

    A. mayas

    B. incas

    C. aztecas

    D. olmecas

102. **Miguel de Cervantes Saavedra mostró el conflicto entre _____ en "Don Quijote".**
    (Rigorous)

    A. realismo y surrealismo

    B. sátira y humor

    C. idealismo y materialismo

    D. el campo y la ciudad

103. **Nicaragua está situada entre ___.**
    (Rigorous)

    A. Honduras y Costa Rica

    B. Costa Rica y Panamá

    C. Guatemala y El Salvador

    D. Guatemala y Belice

104. **El conquistador Hernán Cortés se encontró con el pueblo azteca y ___.**
    (Average Rigor)

    A. lo ayudó

    B. le proporcionó armas

    C. le enseñó a cultivar la tierra

    D. derrotó el imperio que el pueblo había creado

105. Sor Juana Inés de la Cruz (1651-1695) era ___ mexicana.
    (Rigorous)

    A. una artista

    B. una muralista

    C. una poetisa y ensayista

    D. una novelista

106. El pintor Pablo Picasso creó el estilo de arte llamado ___.
    (Average Rigor)

    A. surrealismo

    B. cubismo

    C. impresionismo

    D. realismo

107. ___ ocurrió de 1936 a 1939.
    (Average Rigor)

    A. La Primera Guerra Mundial

    B. La Segunda Guerra Mundial

    C. La Revolución de la Independencia Estadounidense

    D. La Guerra Civil Española

108. El "TLC" se refiere al ___.
    (Rigorous)

    A. Tratado comercial entre los EEUU, Canadá y México (Tratado de Libre Comercio)

    B. Tratado del 16 de septiembre

    C. Tratado de Guadalupe Hidalgo

    D. Tratado Liberal Cubano

109. Tenochtitlán era la capital de los ___.
    (Average Rigor)

    A. aztecas

    B. mayas

    C. zapotecas

    D. incas

110. Diego Rivera era ___.
    (Average Rigor)

    A. un novelista mexicano

    B. un pintor español del período surrealista

    C. un pintor mexicano del período surrealista

    D. un muralista cubano del período surrealista

111. Simón Bolívar fue el primer presidente del ___ independiente de 1824 a 1826.
     (Rigorous)

     A.   Perú

     B.   Ecuador

     C.   Chile

     D.   Venezuela

112. El autor de "Cien años de soledad" es ___.
     (Average Rigor)

     A.   Federico García Lorca

     B.   Gabriel García Márquez

     C.   Salvador Allende

     D.   Octavio Paz

113. ___, el cantante de ópera, nació en México de padres españoles.
     (Easy)

     A.   Diego Rivera

     B.   Julio Iglesias

     C.   Luis Miguel

     D.   Plácido Domingo

114. El gran artista "El Greco", nació en ___.
     (Average Rigor)

     A.   Creta

     B.   Grecia continental

     C.   Cerdeña

     D.   Toledo

115. Andalucía, Cataluña, Galicia y Extremadura son ___.
     (Average Rigor)

     A.   ciudades españolas

     B.   ciudades latinoamericanas

     C.   comunidades autónomas de España

     D.   provincias latinoamericanas

116. El colonialismo tuvo como objetivos principales, ___.
    (Rigorous)

    A. beneficiarse de la desarrollada civilización de algunos pueblos indígenas

    B. agotar los recursos naturales de los países conquistados

    C. convertir los nativos al cristianismo y enseñarlos a luchar

    D. extender el poder y el dominio de los países conquistadores a través de su imperio económico, político y religioso

117. Al recibir una invitación a cenar en España, usted debe preguntar ___.
    (Average Rigor)

    A. ¿Qué va a servir?

    B. ¿A qué hora queréis que llegue?

    C. ¿A qué hora me quieres llegar?

    D. ¿Qué debo llevar?

118. El Salvador, como muchos países en América Central, produce ___.
    (Rigorous))

    A. café y azúcar

    B. café y bananas

    C. azúcar y bananas

    D. maíz y bananas

119. Por lo general, en los países latinoamericanos, se usa el tuteo para hablar con ___.
    (Easy)

    A. profesores y agentes de policía

    B. abogados, médicos y enfermeros

    C. amigos y miembros de la familia

    D. negociantes y empleados de tiendas

120. La ganadora del Premio Nóbel de Literatura, Gabriela Mistral, fue la primera mujer _____.
    (Rigorous)

    A. que ganó el Premio

    B. escritora de España

    C. escritora de América Latina

    D. escritora de lengua indígena

121. La mayoría de la música de latinoamérica es una mezcla de los ritmos ___.
    (Rigorous)

    A. españoles y africanos

    B. españoles y nativos

    C. africanos y nativos

    D. mexicanos y españoles

122. Se puede encontrar el uso muy frecuente del tuteo en ___.
    (Average Rigor)

    A. Argentina y Uruguay

    B. Chile, Cuba, Colombia y la mayoría de los países latinoamericanos

    C. sólo en España

    D. sólo en el Caribe

123. Barcelona es la capital de ___ .
    (Average Rigor)

    A. España

    B. Valencia

    C. Andalucía

    D. Cataluña

124. Se usa el pronombre "vos" en ___.
    (Average Rigor)

    A. España solamente

    B. lecturas y discursos

    C. Argentina, Perú, Chile, Ecuador y en otros países hispanos

    D. antiguas obras literarias

125. Termine el dicho: "Dime con quién andas y ___".
    (Average Rigor)

    A. déjala correr

    B. mona se queda

    C. se lo pondrá

    D. te diré quién eres

INSTRUCTION AND ASSESSMENT

Complete the following statements about foreign language teaching methodology

126. Krashen's Language Acquisition Theory contends that learning and acquisition of language are two distinct processes, with learning being ___.
    (Rigorous)

    A. the natural development of language as seen in children learning their native language

    B. the acquiring of language by the unconscious used in conversation

    C. a censor in one's mind that filters the correct and incorrect language

    D. formal and intentional knowledge about a language

127. The five stages of Cultural Adaptation, or Culture Shock, are ___.
    (Rigorous)

    A. Honeymoon, Disintegration, Re-integration, Autonomy, and Independence

    B. Fear, Coping, Rejection, Acquisition, and Learning

    C. Independence, Autonomy, Disintegration, Re-integration, and Fluency

    D. Inability to communicate, Frustration, Adaptation, Learning, and Fluency

128. A linguistic theory that sees language as the understanding and use of "linguistic units" within sentences describes ___.
    (Rigorous))

    A. the Theory of Discourse Analysis

    B. Pragmatics

    C. The Audio-Lingual Approach

    D. Informal and Off-Hand technique

129. Content-based teaching, also known as the use of authentic materials, consists of ___.
(Rigorous)

   A. the tactile use of authentic cultural objects to reinforce language memory

   B. utilizing texts (passages, novels, articles) from authentic sources within the language. For example, reading a newspaper from Spain

   C. utilizing native speakers in the classroom to converse in, and clarify the language

   D. having the instructor choose, or allowing students to choose subjects that the students have genuine interest in; thereby, encouraging student analysis of these subjects

Choose the item which best describes the following:

130. Language is a set of habits, requiring oral practice of pattern drills and memorized responses. *(Rigorous))*

    A. Grammatical Method

    B. Audio-lingual Method

    C. Natural Approach

    D. Total Physical Response

131. The emphasis is on communicative competence rather than memorizing grammar rules and stressing accuracy. *(Rigorous)*

    A. Grammatical Method

    B. Audio-lingual Method

    C. Natural Approach

    D. Total Physical Response

132. This was originally used to teach Greek and Latin. Students learn elaborate grammar rules and bilingual lists of words. *(Rigorous)*

    A. Grammatical Method

    B. Audio-lingual Method

    C. Natural Approach

    D. Total Physical Response

133. This makes use of oral commands; students demonstrate their comprehension by physically reacting to the content of the message. *(Rigorous)*

    A. Grammatical Method

    B. Audio-lingual Method

    C. Natural Approach

    D. Total Physical Response

READING COMPREHENSION

Read the short passages below and then choose the most accurate response based on your reading.

FEDERICO GARCÍA LORCA

El famoso poeta español, Federico García Lorca, fue asesinado durante la Guerra Civil Española. Fue uno de los miembros más distinguidos de la generación del 27. Su muerte fue trágica para el mundo entero.

García Lorca nació en Fuente Vaqueros, en Granada, el 5 de junio de 1898. Cuando era joven asistió a "la Facultad de Filosofía y Letras" de la ciudad de Córdoba. Pero un poco después, fue a Madrid para seguir sus estudios. Allí conoció a Pablo Picasso, a Salvador Dalí, a Manuel de Falla y a Andrés Segovia. Durante su vida tuvo la oportunidad de pintar, tocar la guitarra, escribir y viajar a Argentina, Cuba y los Estados Unidos.

Desafortunadamente, murió en circunstancias misteriosas el 19 de agosto de 1936; pero, su espíritu y su talento viven hoy a través de su poesía y obras de teatro. Su muerte fue una gran pérdida.

134. **García Lorca estudió en universidades en ___.**
(Easy)

A. Córdoba y Madrid

B. Granada, Córdoba y Madrid

C. Granada y Córdoba

D. Argentina, Cuba, y los Estados Unidos

135. **Se hizo amigo de Picasso, Dalí, de Falla y Segovia en ____.**
(Easy)

A. Granada

B. Córdoba

C. Fuente Vaqueros

D. Madrid

136. La idea principal de este pasaje es que García Lorca ____.
(Average Rigor)

A. viajó mucho

B. murió muy joven

C. fue un escritor con mucho talento y un futuro prometedor

D. tenía muchos amigos

137. Cuando murió, García Lorca tenía ____.
(Easy)

A. 27 años

B. 36 años

C. 38 años

D. 49 años

LA TRAVESÍA DE LA TORMENTA

Hoy por la mañana, los investigadores del Centro Urbano predijeron que la tormenta se alejaría de la costa, aunque cientos de miles de habitantes huyeron de las playas e islas costeras causando un frenético embrollo. Esta tarde, su trayectoria sigue alejándose de la región. La tormenta tenía más de 200 millas de ancho y vientos de 110 millas por hora.

138. **¿Todavía hay una amenaza por la costa?**
 (Rigorous)

 A. Sí, hay un frenético embrollo.

 B. Sí, la tormenta está atravesándola.

 C. No, las playas están lejanas.

 D. No, la tormenta se alejó del área.

139. **¿De qué tipo de fenómeno meteorológico trata la lectura?**
 (Average Rigor)

 A. Un terremoto

 B. Una llovizna

 C. Un tornado

 D. Un huracán

140. **¿Por qué huyó la gente?**
 (Rigorous)

 A. Para estar a salvo

 B. Para ser vulnerable

 C. Para volver a casa

 D. Para ser atravesados por la tormenta

Answer Key

1. – 20. varies	44. A	69. A	94. C	119. C
21. D	45. C	70. D	95. D	120. C
22. C	46. A	71. D	96. D	121. C
23. A	47. C	72. B	97. A	122. B
24. C	48. D	73. B	98. A	123. D
25. B	49. C	74. D	99. C	124. C
26. C	50. D	75. A	100. A	125. D
27. A	51. B	76. C	101. B	126. D
28. C	52. D	77. B	102. C	127. A
29. D	53. C	78. B	103. A	128. A
30. D	54. A	79. A	104. D	129. D
31. B	55. B	80. D	105. C	130. B
32. A	56. D	81. A	106. B	131. C
33. C	57. B	82. C	107. D	132. A
34. A	58. B	83. A	108. A	133. D
35. B	59. A	84. B	109. A	134. A
36. C	60. D	85. D	110. C	135. D
37. C	61. B	86. A	111. A	136. C
38. B	62. B	87. C	112. B	137. C
39. A	63. D	88. B	113. D	138. D
40. A	64. A	89. B	114. A	139. D
41. A	65. D	90. B	115. C	140. A
42. D	66. C	91. C	116. D	
43. A	67. D	92. D	117. B	
	68. B	93. B	118. A	

Rigor Table

	Easy %20	Average Rigor %40	Rigorous %40
Question #	1, 2, 3, 6, 11, 12, 16, 21, 24, 27, 28, 31, 37, 42, 43, 48, 53, 54, 57, 71, 85, 92, 101, 113, 119, 134, 135, 137	5, 7, 9, 10, 14, 15, 22, 23, 26, 33, 34, 39, 41, 46, 50, 51, 56, 58, 59, 62, 65, 69, 70, 73, 74, 76, 77, 78, 79, 80, 81, 82, 84, 87, 89, 93, 94, 96, 98, 99, 100, 104, 106, 107, 109, 110, 112, 114, 115, 117, 122, 123, 124, 125, 136, 139	4, 8, 13, 17, 18, 19, 20, 25, 29, 30, 32, 35, 36, 38, 40, 44, 45, 47, 49, 52, 55, 60, 61, 63, 64, 66, 67, 68, 72, 75, 83, 86, 88, 90, 91, 95, 97, 102, 103, 105, 108, 111, 116, 118, 120, 121, 126, 127, 128, 129, 130, 131, 132, 133, 138, 140

TEACHER CERTIFICATION STUDY GUIDE

Rationales with Sample Questions

Directions: Read each item and select the best response.

SPEAKING SECTION

For this section of the state exam you will be asked to record your answers in Spanish. Follow all directions on the cassette tape provided at the exam site.

Give the following directions in Spanish:

1. **Take out your books. - Saquen sus libros.**
   (Easy)

   "Sacar" is "to take out" or "to pull out" and "Saquen" is appropriate in the Uds. form since the command is being addressed to a group or class.

2. **Pick up your papers and books. – Recojan sus papeles y sus libros.**
   (Easy)

   "Recoger" is "to pick up" or "to collect" and the correct command form of Uds. is "recojan" since one would take the "er" off of the infinitive recoger and replace it with "an" to make the command form of the conjugation.

3. **Write your answers on the blackboard. – Escriban sus respuestas en la pizarra.**
   (Easy)

   The Uds. command form of "escribir" is "escriban" and the command/imperative form is followed here. For "er" and "ir" verbs, the ending is replaced with "an" for Uds. and for "ar" verbs the ending is replaced with "en" for the Uds. form.

4. **Please get into groups of four or five. – Por favor, pónganse en grupos de cuatro o cinco.**
   (Rigorous)

   "Ponerse" is reflexive meaning "to form yourself" or "to make yourself into" and the same Uds. command form is being used. In this case, it is important to remember the "se" comes at the end of the conjugated "poner" and the accent mark appears over the ó because the syllables require it with the reflexive "se" added on.

5. **Complete the following for homework. – Completen lo siguiente de tarea.**
   (Average Rigor)

   The Uds. command of "completar" is "completen". Uds. is addressing the group as "you all".

6. **Hand in your homework. – Entreguen su tarea.**
   (Easy)

   "Entreguen" is the Uds. command form of "entregar", "to hand over" or "to deliver". "Su tarea" is used instead of "sus tareas" since one would not say "your homeworks".

7. **Describe where you went on your last vacation and what you did there. – Describan a dónde fueron en sus últimas vacaciones y lo que hicieron ahí.**
   (Average Rigor)

   The sentence is getting a little more complex, but remains in 3rd person plural Uds. and "sus vacaciones" is in plural to agree with the number of the subject Uds. or "you all".

8. **Explain what sporting event(s) you plan to watch or attend this coming season: with whom, where, and why? – Expliquen cuáles son los eventos deportivos que están planeando mirar o asistir en esta temporada: ¿con quién, dónde y por qué?**
   (Rigorous)

   The Uds. form of "explicar" is "expliquen" taking off the "ar" and adding on the "en." "Cuáles" is the interrogative word asking "which" in plural and with an accent; and "asistir" is used instead of "atender". "Asistir" is used when showing attendance while "atender" means "to attend to".

9. **Narrate and explain how you spent your last major holiday. – Narren y expliquen cómo pasaron su último día de fiesta.**
   (Average Rigor)

   "Narrar" becomes "narren" in Uds. command form and "cómo" retains its accent because it is being used as an interrogative word "how". "Pasaron" is conjugated in Uds. preterite signifying, "what happened" or "what went on" and "día" is singular because the question asks only about the last day or occurrence.

10. **Describe how you will spend your next family celebration. – Describan cómo van a pasar su próxima celebración familiar.**
    (Average Rigor)

    This format is similar to #9, asking about the next celebration.

11. **María, explain what your favorite book is and why. – María, explica cuál es tu libro favorito y por qué.**
    (Easy)

    Here, María is individually being told "to explain". She is being addressed in the "tú" form which is the singular and familiar "you" and takes a different conjugation. The conjugation for "tú" imperative is the regular indicative 3rd person conjugation except for a few irregular exceptions. You can see the difference in "explica".

12. **Paolo, describe your favorite kind of music. – Paolo, describe o habla de tu música favorita.**
    (Easy)

    Paolo is also being addressed in the "tú" command form.

13. **Dave, what hobby would you like to pursue in more depth? Why? – Dave, ¿a qué pasatiempo te gustaría dedicarle más tiempo? ¿Por qué?**
    (Rigorous)

    Dave is being addressed in the "tú" command form with "cuál" as the interrogative word. "Gustar" is in the conditional because there is uncertainty in the future. The conditional is often used with the subjunctive to show doubt or uncertainty.

14. **Lisa, explain a news story you have been following in the paper or on the television. – Lisa, explica un artículo de noticias que hayas leído en el periódico o en la televisión recientemente.**
    (Average Rigor)

    We are using the same "tú" command form for "explica" and "artículo" is used instead of "historia" or "cuento" since they would be referring to a "story" one would read or be told.

15. **Chad, describe a political event or story of importance to you. – Chad, describe un evento o una historia política de importancia para ti.**
    (Average Rigor)

    This follows the same "tú" command form which is the same as the egular, indicative Ud. form of "describir". "Para ti" is used because "tú" can't be used after a preposition and "para" is used as the preposition "for" when "people" and/or "a reason for something" comes after.

16. **Consuelo, where do you live and why do you live there? – Consuelo, ¿dónde vives y por qué vives ahí?**
    (Easy)

    This format is different. Consuelo is simply being asked a question in the familiar you singular, or "tú", form of the indicative. No command form is used.

17. **Latasha, what advice would you like to give to the president about the importance of education funding in the 21st century? – Latasha, ¿qué consejo te gustaría dar al presidente sobre la importancia de fondos educativos en el siglo veintiuno?**
    (Rigorous)

    The format changes again and in this instance, a question is being asked in the conditional form. The conditional "would you like to" shows speculation about the future.

18. **Ben, what do you think about efforts being done to save the environment in your state and in the country in general? Why? – Ben, ¿qué piensas sobre los esfuerzos que se hacen para el medio ambiente en tu estado y en el país en general? ¿Por qué?**
    (Rigorous)

    This question is also asked in the present "tú", form of the indicative, so "pensar" is in the indicative "piensas". "Esfuerzos" are "forces" and "environment" is "medio ambiente".

19. **Manuel, what would you advise students about working long hours after school? Defend your opinion. – Manuel, ¿qué les aconsejarías a los estudiantes sobre el trabajar muchas horas después del colegio? Defiende tu opinión.**
    (Rigorous)

    This question comes in two parts. The first part of the question asks Manuel "what would you advise" in the "tú", form. Since "would" appears in the question, we know this falls into "conditional" conjugation. "Aconsejar" is the verb "to advise" and to make it conditional, one would just add "-ías" for tú" conjugation. The second part of the question is a command and so "defender" is conjugated as "defiende".

20. **Kate, do you think professional athletes should be held to higher standards than other public figures? Why? – Kate, ¿piensas que los deportistas profesionales deberían tener estándares más altos que los de otras figuras públicas? ¿Por qué?**
    (Rigorous)

    This question also shows a duality. "Piensas" is in the present indicative "tú", form but then "should be held" in the second portion of the question is in the conditional. The conjugation is "deberían" referring to the athletes is "deber + ían" for the "ellos" form of the conditional. "¿Por qué?" is correct here because it means "why".

TEACHER CERTIFICATION STUDY GUIDE

LISTENING SECTION

Please note a written script is provided in these sample materials. However, the state examination will not include a written text, written questions, or written choices in this segment of the test.

Listen carefully to the following passages and questions. Answer the following based upon what you heard. (*Audio script is in italics*)

21. **¿Cuál es el propósito del viaje de Rigoberta Menchú a España?** *(Easy)*

    Rigoberta Menchú, una indígena Guatemalteca que nació en 1959, ganó el Premio Nóbel de la Paz en 1992. Viajará a varios países, entre ellos, España. Menchú va a estar en Madrid donde dialogará con el nuevo presidente del gobierno español. Menchú va a discutir las maneras en que sufre la población indígena de América Latina. Rigoberta Menchú ha dedicado sus esfuerzos y trabajo de vida a este grupo.

    ¿Cuál es el propósito del viaje de Rigoberta Menchú a España?

    A. Viajar a varios países europeos

    B. Conocer personalmente al Príncipe Felipe de Borbón

    C. Recibir el Premio Nóbel de la Paz

    D. Hablar sobre sus esfuerzos por las comunidades indígenas

    Answer D. Hablar sobre sus esfuerzos por las comunidades indígenas

    Rigoberta Menchú's life work is to help others without financial gain. She has traveled to many countries to spread her message and has received the Nobel Peace Prize.

22. **¿Qué se destaca en este texto que le gusta al Príncipe Felipe?**
   (Average Rigor)

   El Príncipe Felipe de Borbón, el futuro líder de España, nació en 1968. Estudió en Canadá y en los Estados Unidos. Es muy atlético y se interesa mucho en los deportes. Aunque el príncipe es famoso lleva una vida bastante normal. Está bien preparado para ser el próximo Rey de España, según los políticos europeos.

   ¿Qué se destaca en este texto que le gusta al Príncipe Felipe?

   A. Conversar con los norteamericanos

   B. Visitar las universidades canadienses

   C. Practicar deportes

   D. Visitar ciudades norteamericanas

   Answer C. Practicar deportes

   It is the only answer that is specifically stated in the text. The others are used as descriptive information.

23. **¿Cómo cambió mi estilo de vida?**
    (Average Rigor)

    Antes de obtener mi licencia de conducir yo siempre tenía que depender de otras personas para salir de paseo. No era independiente. No podía salir con mis amigos impulsivamente. Ahora tengo más libertad e independencia.

    ¿Cómo cambió mi estilo de vida?

    A. Radicalmente

    B. Impulsivamente

    C. Solamente

    D. Dependiente

    Answer A. Radicalmente

    "Radicalmente" (radically) is the best answer because it describes how this person's life has changed from being dependent to independent. S/he has not become impulsive; rather there was a big change in his/her life.

24. **¿Adónde van ellos primero?**
   (Easy)

   Por favor, mañana tienes que salir temprano conmigo para ir de compras; porque voy a tener una fiesta el sábado. Espero que haya tortillas en la Bodega García, porque no tengo tiempo para ir al supermercado Solano, lejos en Miami. ¡Ojalá que yo tenga suficiente comida para todos los invitados!

   ¿Adónde van ellos primero?

   A. A una fiesta

   B. Al supermercado

   C. A una bodega

   D. A Miami

   Answer C. A una bodega.

   It explicitly states in the text that she will go to a bodega and does not have time to go to the supermarket located in Miami.

25. ¿Qué deben comprar?
    (Rigorous)

En la sala sólo hay un sillón de cuero y una lámpara; entonces necesitamos un sofá para sentarnos y una televisión para ver nuestros programas favoritos. En el comedor nos falta una mesa grande; aunque hay seis sillas.

¿Qué deben comprar?

- A. Un sillón de cuero y una lámpara
- B. Un sofá, una televisión y una mesa grande
- C. Una mesa grande y seis sillas
- D. No nos falta nada

Answer B. Un sofá, una televisión y una mesa grande

They already have the furnishings listed in A. They have the six chairs but not the large table in C. They do need furniture, so D is incorrect, making B the correct answer.

STRUCTURE OF THE LANGUAGE

Choose the most accurately written item.

26. A. Es necesario que él estudiar.

    B. Es necesario que él estudié.

    C. Es necesario que él estudie.

    D. Es necesario que él estudia.

    (Average Rigor)

    Answer C. Es necesario que él estudie.

    After an impersonal phrase, one must use the subjunctive. A is in the infinitive, B is in the preterite and D is in the present tense.

27. A. Necesito leer el libro.

    B. Necesito que yo leo el libro.

    C. Necesito que yo lea el libro.

    D. Necesito que yo leer el libro.

    (Easy)

    Answer A. Necesito leer el libro.

    After a conjugated verb, if the subject does not change, one must use the infinitive. The "que" is not necessary and neither is the subjunctive.

28. A.   El lápiz de el es azul.

B.   Él lápiz de el es azul.

C.   El lápiz de él es azul.

D.   Él lápiz de él es azul.

(Easy)

Answer C. El lápiz de él es azul.

"El" is the definite article of "lápiz" and so does not require an accent as "él" the pronoun for "he" does.

29. A.   Si tuviera el dinero viajara a Japón.

B.   Si tuviera el dinero viajará a Japón.

C.   Si tuviera el dinero viajaré a Japón.

D   Si tuviera el dinero viajaría a Japón.

(Rigorous)

Answer D. Si tuviera el dinero viajaría a Japón.

This is the basic hypothetical construction. Si + past subjunctive + conditional. If I had money (I do not), I would travel to Japan. D is the only answer that follows this grammatical structure. "Si" indicates doubt or condition and "tuviera" is in the imperfect subjunctive, setting viajar up for the conditional "viajaría", "could travel".

TEACHER CERTIFICATION STUDY GUIDE

30. A.   ¡Que pena que él se fuera!

  B.   ¡Qué pena que él se fue!

  C.   ¡Que pena qué él se fue!

  D.   ¡Qué pena que él se fuera!

(Rigorous)

Answer D. ¡Qué pena que él se fuera!

"Qué" with an accent is used for exclamatory or interrogative sentences. The subjunctive is used with "ir" because "pena" expresses an emotion.

31. A.   ¿Porque lo hiciste tú?

  B.   ¿Por qué lo hiciste tú?

  C   .¿Por qué lo hiciste tu?

  D. ¿Porque lo hiciste tu?

(Easy)

Answer B. ¿Por qué lo hiciste tú?

"Porque" is not an interrogative word here. it means "because". "Tu" is a possessive pronoun, not a subject. The answer is B because it uses the interrogative word "why" (por qué) and refers to the subject "tú" agreeing with the conjugated verb "hiciste".

32. A. Se prohibe fumar.

B. El fumar es prohibido.

C. La fumar es prohibido.

D. Fumando es prohibido.

(Rigorous)

Answer A. Se prohibe fumar.

The gerund "fumando" is not used, and although in many cases it is appropriate to use "the definite article + infinitive" construction to act as a gerund, the correct answer is A. The general 3rd person passive reflexiveis used to denote a general "People are prohibited to smoke," without a specific subject, or the impersonal tense "Smoking is prohibited".

33. A. Además de leer, me gusta nadando.

B. Además de leyendo, me gusta nadando.

C. Además de leer, me gusta nadar.

D. Además de leyendo, me gusta nadar.

(Average Rigor)

Answer C. Además de leer, me gusta nadar.

The infinitive is used when following the preposition "de".

34. A. Nos gusta esquiar y navegar.

B. Nos gustamos esquiar y navegar.

C. Nos gusta esquiando y navegando.

D. Nos gusta esquiar e navegar.

(Average Rigor)

Answer A. Nos gusta esquiar y navegar.

"Gustar" is only conjugated into the 3rd person singular and plural, eliminating B. An infinitive must follow the conjugation of "gustar", eliminating C. "e" is only used if the following word begins with the letter "i" or "hi", making A the correct answer.

35. A. Se me olvidé la cartera.

B. Se me olvidó la cartera.

C. Me la olvidó la cartera.

D. Me la olvidé la cartera.

(Rigorous)

Answer B. Se me olvidó la cartera.

The use of "se" is to show causality and to relieve the speaker of responsibility. "Olvidar" is a reflexive verb and "olvidarse" is being used in the passive reflexive voice.

36. A. Cuando regresamos de México vamos a mostrarle las fotos.

   B. Cuando regresemos de México vamos a mostrarle los fotos.

   C. Cuando regresemos de México vamos a mostrarle las fotos.

   D. Cuando regresamos de México vamos a mostrarle los fotos.

   (Rigorous)

   Answer C. Cuando regresemos de México vamos a mostrarle las fotos.

   "Cuando", or "when", in this case refers to the future. Since the action has not happened, it is hypothetical and the subjunctive must be used. "Fotos" is short for "fotografías" and the feminine plural article, "las", must be used.

37. A. Los regalos son para tú.

   B. Los regalos son para tu.

   C. Los regalos son para ti.

   D. Los regalos son para te.

   (Easy)

   Answer C. Los regalos son para ti.

   The second person subject pronoun ("tú") cannot follow a preposition and the prepositional pronoun "ti" must be used.

TEACHER CERTIFICATION STUDY GUIDE

38. A. En mí opinión, la gente es muy buena.

    B. En mi opinión, la gente es muy buena.

    C. En mi opinión, la gente son muy buena.

    D. En mí opinión, la gente son muy buena.

(Rigorous)

Answer B. En mi opinión, la gente es muy buena.

"Mí" is a prepositional pronoun and should not be used as a possessive pronoun. Before "opinion", "mi" must be used. "La gente" is singular 3rd person even though it represents a collective. In English it is said that "people are", but in Spanish, "gente" is treated and conjugated as 3rd person singular like "él", "ella" or "grupo" so it takes "es" as the conjugated verb of "ser". Therefore, B is the best answer.

39. A. ¿Viste a Mónica y a Carmen?

    B. ¿Viste Mónica a Carmen?

    C. ¿Viste a Mónica Carmen?

    D. ¿Viste Mónica y Carmen?

(Average Rigor)

Answer A. ¿Viste a Mónica y a Carmen?

Before a person's name, one must use the personal "a". Therefore, to ask if you saw Mónica and Carmen, you must place the personal "a " before each name.

40. A. Se puso la chaqueta por el frío.

B. Se puso la chaqueta como el frío.

C. Puso la chaqueta por el frío.

D. Puso la chaqueta para el frío.

(Rigorous)

Answer A. Se puso la chaqueta por el frío.

"Poner" is reflexive in this case because s/he is putting on the jacket. "Por" is correct because it is expressing a cause/motive. "Por" literally means "because of" here. Literally, (because of) the cold, s/he is putting on the jacket.

Choose the correct response or most appropriate rejoinder:

41. ¿Quién lo hizo?
    (Average Rigor)

    A.   –Yo lo hice.

    B.   –Yo me hice.

    C.   –Yo lo hizo.

    D.   –Me lo hizo.

    Answer A. Yo lo hice.

    The question asks, "Who did it?" in 3rd person singular preterite. A is the best answer because the subject pronoun (yo) agrees with the conjugated verb (hice). To respond to the question, one must use the direct object making A the correct answer. Moreover, the direct object "lo" is kept before the verb and "hice" is an irregular conjugation in the 1st person preterite of the verb "hacer". B uses the reflexive form of "hacer" which is incorrect.

42. ¿Cuándo estudiaste para el examen?
    (Easy)

    A.   –Estudió anoche por dos horas.

    B.   –Estudio anoche por dos horas.

    C.   –Estudiaste anoche por dos horas.

    D.   –Estudié anoche por dos horas.

    Answer D. Estudié anoche por dos horas.

    When the question is directed in the second person singular, the first person singular must respond. "Estudié" is the first person singular conjugation in the preterite.

43. **Él habla tres idiomas.**
    (Easy)

    A. –¡Qué bien que habla tres idiomas!

    B. –¡Qué bien que hable tres idiomas!

    C. –¡Qué bien que hablo tres idiomas!

    D. –¡Qué bien que hablas tres idiomas!

    Answer A. ¡Qué bien que habla tres idiomas!

    The response requires the 3rd person singular form of the verb because it is talking about "él". The subjunctive is not needed because "qué bien" is not a complete structure that needs the subjunctive.

44. **Me dolía la cabeza la semana pasada.**
    (Rigorous)

    A. –¿Fue al médico?

    B. –¿Fue el médico?

    C. –¿Iba el médico?

    D. –¿Fuiste el médico?

    Answer A. ¿Fue al médico?

    "Me dolía" is in the imperfect of the verb "doler" or "dolerse" since the headache lasted over a period of time last week; but, the visit to the doctor was a specific time and action, so the answer was in the preterite. It was addressed to "you" the 3rd person formal "Ud." form of "ser". After the verb "ir" one must use the preposition "a" to show movement toward, "to go to". That is how we get "al". It is the conjunction of "a" + "el" = "al". Therefore A is the answer since it is the only option that shows this correct construction.

TEACHER CERTIFICATION STUDY GUIDE

45. ¿Lo conociste en el colegio?
    (Rigorous)

    A. –Sí, lo conoció allí.

    B. –Sí, me conocí allí.

    C. –Sí, lo conocí allí.

    D. –Sí, me lo conoció allí.

    Answer C. Sí, lo conocí allí.

    The question is asked in the form of "Ud.". "Did you meet him in high school?" So, it must be answered with the first person singular, using the same direct object "lo" before the conjugated verb. B cannot be the answer because the verb is not used in the reflexive and does not reiterate the direct object. So C is correct, "I met him there".

46. **Nosotras hemos_____ una novela.**
    (Average Rigor)

    A. Escrito

    B. Escribido

    C. Escribida

    D. Escrita

    Answer A. Escrito

    "Escrito" is the irregular past participle of the verb "escribir." Answer B follows the formation pattern of regular "ir" verbs, but is incorrect. Given the feminine subject, it might appear that the participle would also be feminine (i.e. "escrita"); however, past participles do not agree with the subject in gender or number.

47. Mi tía ha _____ muy joven.
    (Rigorous)

    A. Morido

    B. Muerta

    C. Muerto

    D. Morida

    Answer C. Muerto

    "Muerto" is the irregular past participle of the verb "morir." Answer A follows the formation pattern of regular "ir" verbs, but is incorrect, as is Answer D "morida". "Muerta" may appear as a logical choice in that the past participle is formed correctly and takes a feminine ending; however, past participles do not agree with the subject in gender or number.

48. ¿Cuándo prepararás la comida?
    (Easy)

    A. La preparé mañana.

    B. La prepararás mañana.

    C. La prepara mañana.

    D. La prepararé mañana.

    Answer D. La prepararé mañana.

    The question is asked in second person "tú" future tense, indicating that the first person singular will answer the question in the future tense. Option A is conjugated in the preterite. Option B is in the future but conjugated in the second person singular. Option C is in the past subjunctive, so D is the correct answer. The future tense = infinitive + é for 1st person singular.

49. Change the following sentence to passive voice: "María compró la pintura de Dalí."
    (Rigorous)

    A. La pintura de Dalí es comprada por María.

    B. La pintura de Dalí se compra por María.

    C. La pintura de Dalí fue comprada por María.

    D. La pintura de Dalí se compró por María.

    Answer C. La pintura de Dalí fue comprada por María.

    The main sentence is written in the active voice of the preterite tense so changing the sentence to the passive voice must also be in the preterite. That automatically eliminates Answers A and B. Answer D is also incorrect since the passive voice is formed using the verb "ser."

50. *(Average Rigor)*

    A. ¿Mira Ud. al espejo cuando peinarse?

    B. ¿Se mira Ud. al espejo cuando peina?

    C. ¿Ud. mirase al espejo cuando peina?

    D. ¿Se mira Ud. al espejo cuando se peina?

    Answer D. ¿Se mira Ud. al espejo cuando se peina?

    There are two reflexive actions in the sentence so the response eliminates all answers except D. The question is about a person looking at him/herself in a mirror while combing his/her hair. That is the reason why both verbs must use the reflexive form.

51. *(Average Rigor)*

    A. Mis clases son bastantes difíciles, pero tengo mucha gente que me ayuda.

    B. Mis clases son bastante difíciles, pero tengo mucha gente que me ayuda.

    C. Mis clases son bastante difícil, pero tengo mucha gente que me ayuda.

    D. Mis clases son bastantes difíciles, pero tengo mucho gente que me ayuda.

    Answer B. Mis clases son bastante difíciles, pero tengo mucha gente que me ayuda.

    The adverb "bastante" does not agree in gender or number with the feminine plural subject of the sentence "clases" as it is invariable and does not change form. Answer C is incorrect because "difícil" is an adjective that modifies the subject "clases" and must agree with this feminine plural noun.

52. Choose the correct adverbial combination to complete the following sentence:
    (Rigorous)

    Tenemos problemas políticos y sociales. Necesitamos mejorar_____.

    A. politicamente y socialmente

    B. políticamente y socialmente

    C. política y sociálmente

    D. política y socialmente

    Answer D. política y socialmente

    Answers A and B can automatically be eliminated since when placed in succession within a sentence (if the two adverbs are typically formed using "mente,") the first adverb drops the "mente." Answer C is incorrect since any adverb written with "mente" respects the original accent found in the adjectival form. Since "social" as an adjective does not carry an accent, an accent is not added when transformed into an adverb with "mente."

53. *(Easy)*

    A. Esto lo hizo Juan o Oscar.

    B. Esto lo hizo Juan e Oscar.

    C. Miguel e Inés juegan al balón.

    D. Miguel y Inés juegan al balón.

    Answer C. Miguel e Inés juegan al balón.

    Conjunctions "o" and "y" change respectively to "u" and "e" for phonetic reasons when the following word begins with the same vowel sound. Only in Answer C was the conjunction changed from "y" to "e."

54. (Easy)

A. Habla del niño.

B. Habla a el niño.

C. Habla de el niño.

D. Habla en el niño.

Answer A. Habla del niño.

To combine "de" and "el", "del" must be used. None of the other contractions are correct.

55. Si un español dice: "Me gusta comer palomitas en mi coche", un argentino diría:
(Rigorous)

A. Me gusta comer pochoclos en mi coche.

B. Me gusta comer pochoclos en mi auto.

C. Me gusta comer porotos en mi carro.

D. Me gusta comer cabritas en mi carro.

Answer B. Me gusta comer pochoclos en mi auto.

The words "palomitas" and "coche" in Argentina are "pochoclos" and "auto" respectively. "Porotos" and "cabritas" in Chile mean "beans" and "popcorn."

56. Choose the correct written form for the numerical expression "551 bombillas."
    (Average Rigor)

    A. Quinientos, cincuenta y uno

    B. Quinientas cincuentaiuno

    C. Quinientas y cincuenta y una

    D. Quinientas cincuenta y una

    Answer D. Quinientas cincuenta y una

    The numeral adjective must agree with the noun it modifies. That would eliminate Answer A since "bombillas" is feminine. Answer B with "cincuentaiuno" is incorrect in that "y" must be used to join "cincuenta" with "uno." Answer C is incorrect as the numbers that follow "quinientas" are not joined using "y".

57. Choose the correct written form of the date.
    (Easy)

    A. 14 de Febrero, 1999

    B. 14 de febrero de 1999

    C. Febrero, 14 de 1999

    D. 14, febrero de 1999

    Answer B. 14 de febrero de 1999

    Dates are written in the order of day, month, year, all in lower case.

58. Choose the correct idiomatic expression.
    (Average Rigor)

    Miguel saludó a Rosa en la escalera, pero ella no se dio cuenta porque es muy despistada;…

    A. siempre anda en los sueños.

    B. siempre anda en la luna.

    C. siempre está en el aire.

    D. siempre está en Marte.

    Answer B. siempre anda en la luna.

    This is the closest idiomatic expression to the meaning of "depistada."

59. **Pedro quería decirnos algo, pero daba tantos detalles que al final le dije:…**
    (Average Rigor)

    A. –¡Basta, ve al grano!

    B. –¡Basta, ve al centro!

    C. –¡Basta, ve al núcleo!

    D. –¡Basta, ve al punto!

    Answer A. ¡Basta, ve al grano!

    The listener wanted Pedro to get to the point and cut out the unnecessary details. Although Answers B and D could be understood, common idiomatic usage for this situation dictates the choice of Answer A.

TEACHER CERTIFICATION STUDY GUIDE

60. Choose the correct response.

    Hay seis chicas en la clase. Juana tiene 1.80 m. de altura. Todas las otras chicas tienen menos. Juana es _____ la clase.
    (Rigorous)

    A. la menos alta de

    B. más alta que

    C. la más alta que

    D. la más alta de

    Answer D. la más alta de

    This is an example of the absolute superlative so "de" must be used. Juana is the tallest in the class. She is not being compared equally with anyone else in the class or "que" would be used.

61. **Luis tiene muchas fotos. Enrique tiene muchas fotos también.**
    (Rigorous)

    A. Luis tiene menos fotos que Enrique.

    B. Enrique tiene tantas fotos como Luis.

    C. Enrique tiene más fotos que Luis.

    D. Enrique tiene tantas fotos que Luis.

    Answer B. Enrique tiene tantas fotos como Luis.

    Answers A and C are grammatically correct, but are not the correct answers based on the two statements that were made about Luis and Enrique. Answer D is incorrect in that the comparative form is "tanto como," not "tanto que."

62. **Me importan los asuntos de los que habíamos hablado.**
    (Average Rigor)

    A. A mí me importan tampoco.

    B. A mí me importan también.

    C. A mí me importan tambien.

    D. A mí me importan tampoco.

    Answer B. A mí me importan también.

    "También" is used to be in agreement in a positive statement. "Tampoco" is used to agree in a negative statement. "También" means "also" while "tampoco" signifies "either" or "neither". "También" always carries an accent over the "e".

Choose the rule or explanation that best explains the following:

63. **Esta mañana Lisette tomaba el sol y yo me bañaba en el mar.**
    (Rigorous)

    A. Incorrect: The two verbs should be in the preterite because the actions occurred at a specific time.

    B. Incorrect: The subordinate verb should be in the preterite tense to contrast the two main events.

    C. Incorrect: The use of "bañarse" is not appropriate.

    D. Correct: The imperfect tense can be used to describe two or more actions going on at the same time in the past.

    Answer D. Correct: The imperfect tense can be used to describe two or more actions going on at the same time in the past.

    The actions were not defined in a specific time frame so the imperfect tense should be used. The preterite is not necessary to contrast the actions because they were performed simultaneously. The imperfect is used when two actions are going on at the same time; and the imperfect is used when one action starts and then another follows. "Bañarse" is used correctly in the statement.

64. **Eran las 2:00 cuando salimos ayer por la tarde.**
    (Rigorous)

    A. Correct: The imperfect tense is used to tell time in the past.

    B. Incorrect: Both verbs should be in the imperfect to describe past actions.

    C. Incorrect: The preterite tense is used to tell time in the past.

    D. Correct: Both verbs are in the imperfect tense to tell a story.

    Answer A. Correct: The imperfect tense is used to tell time in the past.

    The imperfect is used to tell time. The preterite is used with "salir" because the action occurred at a specific time. Therefore A is the only possible selection.

65. **Trabajamos para dos horas.**
    (Average Rigor)

    A. Correct: "Para" is used to indicate a deadline.

    B. Correct: "Para" is used to indicate a length of time.

    C. Incorrect: "Por" is used to indicate a specific hour.

    D. Incorrect: "Por" is used to indicate a length of time.

    Answer D. Incorrect: "Por" is used to indicate a length of time.

    "Por" is used to indicate a length of time (only in America), two hours. D is correct and not C because "dos horas" is not a specific hour; rather it is a general time period.

66. **Si hubiera más casas baratas, podría comprar una en vez de alquilar.**
    (Rigorous)

    A. Correct: This is the correct form of the pluperfect and imperfect subjunctive.

    B. Incorrect: The subjunctive and conditional forms cannot be combined in a sentence.

    C. Correct: The "si" clause using the imperfect subjunctive can be used with the conditional in the following clause.

    D. Incorrect: "Hubiera" needs a past participle.

    Answer C. Correct: The "si" clause using the imperfect subjunctive can be used with the conditional in the following clause.

    The "si" clause denotes "if" which denotes a possibility or condition – an "if…, then…" statement, making the subjunctive appropriate. Since the action has been ongoing, the imperfect subjunctive is used. This allows for the conditional to be used in the following clause, since there is an element of uncertainty, or condition, throughout.

67. **Estaban viendo la televisión cuando alguien cerró la puerta.**
    (Rigorous)

    A. Incorrect: The imperfect tense is used to tell a story.

    B. Incorrect: The imperfect tense is used to indicate past actions.

    C. Correct: The imperfect tense is used to describe the past.

    D. Correct: The imperfect tense sets the stage for another action to take place.

    Answer D. Correct: The imperfect tense sets the stage for another action to take place.
    The imperfect and preterite tenses are used to describe the past. The preterite is used to show a distinction from an ongoing action or setting (imperfect) to something that has only occurred once or has occurred at a specific time. The imperfect and preterite can be used in the same sentence when the imperfect is used in the first clause and preterite in the second, for the purpose of the imperfect setting up the action of the preterite against a background of continuing action. Therefore, D is the correct answer because "estaban viendo" is setting the storyline and "cerró" interrupts it.

68. **Quisiera que ella lo hiciera.**
    (Rigorous)

    A. Correct: The imperfect subjunctive is used following the preterite.

    B. Correct: The imperfect subjunctive is used following a past subjunctive.

    C. Incorrect: The imperfect subjunctive is used to express doubt in the past.

    D. Correct: The imperfect subjunctive is used to express emotion in the past.

    Answer B. Correct: The imperfect subjunctive is used following a past subjunctive.
    Since the statement begins with the imperfect subjunctive and with a verb of desire, the subordinate verb must be in the imperfect subjunctive as a past action. The imperfect subjunctive is used after a main, noun clause using the imperfect, preterite, past perfect or conditional.

69. **Música es el idioma universal.**
    (Average Rigor)

    A. Incorrect: The definite article is needed with nouns to point out a specific person or thing and is used with nouns expressing an abstract or generalized concept.

    B. Incorrect: The word "idioma" is feminine.

    C. Correct: The word "música" is too general a concept to be labeled "la música".

    D. Correct: The verb "ser" is used to define.

    Answer A. Incorrect: The definite article is needed with nouns to point out a specific person or thing and is used with nouns expressing an abstract or generalized concept.

    To express a generality, one must use the definite article. A is the correct answer because the definite article needs to be placed before a noun that is described in a general or ambiguous way – like an idea, a concept, or in this case, "música". "Ser" is used correctly and the word "idioma" is masculine.

TEACHER CERTIFICATION STUDY GUIDE

70. **Señora Cabrices es de Caracas, Venezuela.**
    (Average Rigor)

    A. Correct: The verb "ser" is used to express origin or nationality.

    B. Correct: The preposition "a" is not needed.

    C. Incorrect: The verb "estar" is used to express location.

    D. Incorrect: The definite article should precede the title of someone's name.

    Answer D. Incorrect: The definite article should precede the title of someone's name.

    If one is not directly addressing a person, the definite article must be used before a person's title.

71. **Mis hermanos y yo somos altas.**
    (Easy)

    A. Correct: The verb "ser" is used to describe physical attributes.

    B. Correct: The compound subject requires the verb "somos".

    C. Correct: The possessive pronoun should be in the plural form.

    D. Incorrect: The plural adjective should be in the masculine plural form.

    Answer D. Incorrect: The plural adjective should be in the masculine plural form.

    The sentence as a whole is incorrect because the plural adjective is incorrect. If feminine and masculine subjects are used, a group of mixed or unknown gender, the adjective used to describe them together must be in the masculine form and agree in number.

72. ¿Quién es? ¿Será la niñera?
    (Rigorous)

    A. Incorrect: The future tense is not used to respond to a question in the present.

    B. Correct: The future tense is used to indicate probability.

    C. Correct: The subject is understood.

    D. Incorrect: The subject should precede the verb.

    Answer B. Correct: The future tense is used to indicate probability.

    If the person answering a question is not 100% positive of the response; s/he uses the future tense to express the probability of his/her answer with doubt. The future tense may respond to a question in the present showing probability.

73. La problema principal es que no han hecho nada.
    (Average Rigor)

    A. Correct: Most nouns ending in "ma" are feminine.

    B. Incorrect: Not all of words ending in "ma" are feminine.

    C. Correct: The word "no" precedes the present perfect construction.

    D. Correct: Spanish requires the double negative.

    Answer B. Incorrect: Most nouns ending in "ma" are masculine.

    Although the double negative is frequently used in Spanish, it is not required here. The best answer is B, because words that end in "ma" are normally masculine. By using the feminine article, the sentence is incorrect.

74. **Mi padre es pesimista pero mi madre es optimista.**
    (Average Rigor)

    A. Incorrect: Adjectives should agree in both gender and number with the noun they modify.

    B. Incorrect: The conjunction "sino" should be used in the negative construction.

    C. Correct: The subjunctive mood is not needed to express an opinion.

    D. Correct: Adjectives that end in "ista" have only one singular form for masculine and feminine nouns.

    Answer D. Correct: Adjectives that end in "ista" have only one singular form for masculine and feminine nouns.

    The adjectives agree with the nouns they modify in this sentence, because the adjectives that end in –ista do not distinguish between genders. There is only one form, therefore the sentence is correct. "Sino" is used in negative constructions, which do not apply here.

75. **Si irás conmigo, será mejor.**
    (Rigorous)

    A. Incorrect: The future tense is never used in the "si" clause.

    B. Correct: The future tense is always used in the "si" clause.

    C. Correct: The future tense is used to express probability.

    D. Correct: The "si" clause denotes more of a probability than a possibility.

    Answer A. Incorrect: The future tense is never used in the "si" clause.

    The future tense is not used with the "si" clause because "si", or "if", expresses doubt or condition, and that would not be appropriate with the future tense. The future tense asserts what will happen (most likely) and not what could happen. The "si" clause would, therefore, be more appropriate with the conditional or subjunctive.

76. ¿Saben ustedes cómo tocar el piano?
    (Average Rigor)

    A. Incorrect: "Como" used in a question requires a written accent mark.

    B. Incorrect: "Saber" is used to indicate the knowledge of a fact.

    C. Incorrect: "Saber" when used to indicate knowledge of how to do something does not require the word "cómo."

    D. Correct: "Tocar" is used to play a musical instrument and "jugar" is used to play a sport or game.

    Answer C. "Saber" when used to indicate knowledge of how to do something does not require the word "cómo."

    "Tocar" is used correctly but the best answer is C because the statement is not correct due to the use of "cómo". "Cómo" does take an accent mark, but this word is not needed after the verb "saber", which indicates knowing facts, skills, etc. Only the infinitive is needed after "saber".

77. Quiero que él lo haga.
    (Average Rigor)

    A. Correct: Object pronouns are attached to affirmative direct commands.

    B. Correct: Object pronouns precede a conjugated verb in both the indicative and subjunctive moods.

    C. Incorrect: The present subjunctive is formed by dropping the "o" of the first person singular present indicative of regular verbs.

    D. Incorrect: The subjunctive is used to express an implied command.

    Answer B. Correct: Object pronouns precede a conjugated verb in both the indicative and subjunctive moods.

    Object pronouns are only attached to the end of verbs when they are in command form, infinitive form or present participles. Answer B is correct because "lo" should precede "haga". Object pronouns usually precede the conjugated verb aside from the exceptions mentioned. The construction of the subjunctive is correct in the subordinate clause.

78. **Se venden muchos autos aquí.**
    (Average Rigor)

    A. Correct: "Se" is used to express an unknown plural subject "they."

    B. Correct: The verb is plural to agree with the plural object.

    C. Incorrect: "Se" is used to denote a reflexive action.

    D. Incorrect: "Se" is only used with the third person singular form of the verb, not the plural.

    Answer B. Correct: The verb is plural to agree with the plural object.

    In this example, "se" is not reflexive but it is in impersonal passive voice. "Se" in general can be used both with the third person singular and plural form of the verb. "Se" does not express the plural subject of "they", "ellos". Instead, it is an impersonal tense, used for the 3rd person plural conjugation of a verb with an unknown plural subject. B is correct. The plural form "venden" is used to agree with the plural object (autos).

79. **¡Tú dime la verdad!**
    Average Rigor)

    A. Correct: "Tú" is a subject pronoun requiring an accent mark.

    B. Correct: "Dar" is an irregular verb when conjugated in the "tú" command form.

    C. Incorrect: The direct and indirect object pronouns should both be attached to the end of the verb "di".

    D. Incorrect: The direct object pronoun should precede the verb."

    Answer A. Correct: "Tú" is a subject pronoun requiring an accent mark.

    "Tú" is a subject pronoun "you" that requires an accent when used as such. When used as a possessive pronoun, the accent is not used, so A is the correct answer. Answer B is incorrect since the verb being conjugated is "decir" and there is only a direct object pronoun "me" and it is appropriate to put it at the end of a verb in command form; therefore, C and D are both incorrect as well.

80. **No lo han leído.**
    (Average Rigor)

    A. Incorrect: The object pronoun precedes the past participle.

    B. Incorrect: The past participle should be plural to agree in number with the subject.

    C. Incorrect: The past participle does not require a written accent mark.

    D. Correct: The object pronoun precedes the entire verb phase.

    Answer D. Correct: The object pronoun precedes the entire verb phase.

    The past participle never agrees in number and gender when it is preceded by the verb "haber", creating the past perfect tense. Therefore, the object pronoun must precede the whole verb construction, making D the only correct answer.

81. **¿Qué es esto?**
    (Average Rigor)

    A. Correct: "Esto" is a neuter demonstrative pronoun and does not take a written accent mark.

    B. Correct: When demonstrative adjectives replace a noun they are called demonstrative pronouns.

    C. Incorrect: "Esto" requires a written accent mark.

    D. Incorrect: Demonstrative pronouns are used to point out.

    Answer A. Correct: "Esto" is a neuter demonstrative pronoun and does not take a written accent mark.

    The neuter demonstrative pronoun never carries an accent. Since the noun is unknown, the neuter demonstrative is used.

82. Vendimos nuestra antigua casa hace muchos años.
    (Average Rigor)

    A. Incorrect: Only quantitative adjectives can precede a noun.

    B. Incorrect: Only qualitative adjectives can precede a noun.

    C. Correct: The meaning of "antigua" in this context is to denote the former home.

    D. Correct: The meaning of "antigua" is this context is to denote the very, very, old home.

    Answer C. The meaning of "antigua" in this context is to denote the former home.

    If the adjective precedes the noun, its meaning is slightly altered. "Antigua" before the noun is "former" and "antigua" after the noun means old.

83. Estábamos yendo al museo de la Reina Sofía a las dos.
    (Rigorous)

    A. Incorrect: The present indicative would be more appropriate than the imperfect.

    B. Incorrect: The correct present participle for "ir" is "iendo".

    C. Incorrect: The verb "ir" should be in the preterite "nosotros" form "fuimos".

    D. Correct: "A" + "el" form the contraction "al" before "museo".

    Answer A. Incorrect: The present indicative would be more appropriate than the imperfect.

    Since the group is going to the museum at two, it indicates that it is a present action, which makes the present indicative, or "vamos" appropriate for the sentence.

84. **Raúl se comió el pollo.**
    (Average Rigor)

    A. Incorrect: The object should precede the subject of the sentence.

    B. Correct: The verb agrees with the subject of the sentence.

    C. Incorrect: The verb "comer" is not reflexive.

    D. Correct: The verb is in the singular to agree with the object of the sentence.

    Answer B. The verb agrees with the subject of the sentence.

    "Comer" can be reflexive and the meaning then changes from "comer" "to eat" to "comerse" "to devour". The "se" refers to Raúl eating the entire chicken rather than a piece of it. Verbs are not conjugated to agree with the object of the sentence, rather the subject.

85. **Él es un buen estudiante.**
    (Easy)

    A. Incorrect: The qualitative adjective should not precede the noun.

    B. Correct: The verb "estar" implies a temporary quality or condition.

    C. Incorrect: The indefinite article is not used with an occupation.

    D. Correct: The adjective "bueno" is shortened before a singular masculine noun.

    Answer D. Correct: The adjective "bueno" is shortened before a singular masculine noun.

    The qualitative adjective can precede the noun in the cases of "bueno" and "malo" and certain others are allowed to precede the noun. "Bueno" is shortened from "bueno" to "buen" when preceding a singular, masculine noun. The indefinite article is used when the noun is modified and "es" derives from the verb "ser" and not "estar", so D is the correct answer.

86. **Se me perdieron los libros.**
    (Rigorous)

    A. Correct: The "me" is used here as an indirect object pronoun.

    B. Incorrect: The verb should agree in number with the subject of the sentence.

    C. Correct: The "me" is used here as a reflexive pronoun.

    D. Incorrect: The word "se" is not needed with the verb "perder."

    Answer A. Correct: The "me" is used here as an indirect object pronoun.

    This is an example of a passive reflexive construction with "libros" as the subject and "me" as the object. Literally translated it would be "The books were lost to me". "Me" is used to relieve the person speaking from responsibility of losing the books.

87. **Anoche estuve enfermo.**
    (Average Rigor)

    A. Incorrect: The preterite describes a specific action or event in the past.

    B. Correct: The imperfect describes an emotional activity in the past.

    C. Correct: The preterite can be used to emphasize that an action has ended.

    D. Incorrect: The imperfect expresses a temporary condition in the past.

    Answer C. Correct: The preterite can be used to emphasize that an action has ended.

    The preterite is appropriate here since "anoche" marks a specific time frame, last night, hat the speaker was sick. The action took place, but has since ended.

88. **Ayer iba al cine cuando vino Diego.**
    (Rigorous)

    A. Correct: The imperfect describes a past repetitive action.

    B. Correct: The imperfect stresses an action in progress when another action took place.

    C. Incorrect: The preterite is needed to express a past fact.

    D. Incorrect: The preterite expresses an action that took place at a definite time in the past.

    Answer B. Correct: The imperfect stresses an action in progress when another action took place.

    The imperfect is used when two actions are occurring simultaneously or when one begins after another is already in motion; so, although the options specify certain true functions of the preterite and imperfect tenses, only B accurately describes the methods used in this example. The speaker was going to the movies, creating an ongoing action which was interrupted when Diego arrived.

89. **Ella es mayor que yo.**
    (Average Rigor)

    A. Correct: Implies she is physically bigger than I am.

    B. Correct: Implies she is older than I am.

    C. Incorrect: Implies she is the oldest of all.

    D. Incorrect: Implies she is greater than I am.

    Answer B. Correct: Implies she is older than I am.

    "Mayor" means older, making B the only correct response.

90. **Hay más que veinte personas.**
    (Rigorous)

    A. Correct: The comparative requires a written accent.

    B. Incorrect: When this comparison is followed by a number the form is "más de".

    C. Correct: The numeral 20 requires "más de" but not the written form of the number.

    D. Incorrect: The correct comparative is "mayor" for greater than.

    Answer B. Incorrect: When this comparison is followed by a number the form is "mas de".

    Regardless of how the number is written, when one wants to say the exact number, one must use the construction "más de" with the accent. This signifies "more than ..."

91. **Por favor, René, el carro está sucio. Lávalo.**
    (Rigorous)

    A. Incorrect: The command form is not needed here. It is a request.

    B. Incorrect: The object pronoun should precede the conjugated verb.

    C. Correct: The affirmative command is in the familiar form.

    D. Correct: The negative familiar command takes the same form as the second person singular.

    Answer C. Correct: The affirmative command is in the familiar form.

    Even though, "por favor" is used, "Lávalo" is a command using the familiar positive command conjugation of lavar, "lava". The object pronoun, in this case "lo", is always attached to the verb when conjugated in the positive command form and there is no infinitive. The negative familiar command does not have the same form as the second person singular and there are no negative commands in this example. Therefore, choice C is the most appropriate answer.

TEACHER CERTIFICATION STUDY GUIDE

92. **Isabel me conocía por primera vez en 1992.**
    (Easy)

    A. Correct: The verb "conocer" denotes knowing a person.

    B. Correct: The verb "saber" denotes factual knowledge.

    C. Correct: The imperfect of "conocer" implies met for the first time.

    D. Incorrect: The preterite of "conocer" implies met for the first time.

    Answer D. Incorrect: The preterite of "conocer" implies met for the first time.

    Meeting someone for the first time is an action that happens once and at a specific time, thereby needing the preterite. The imperfect is wrong here because meeting someone is not a continuous action. "Conocer" is used to talk about knowing a person but its use in the preterite means to meet (as in for the first time) making option D the correct response.

93. **El agua es pura.**
    (Average Rigor)

    A. Correct: The word "agua" is masculine.

    B. Correct: "El" is used although the word "agua" is feminine.

    C. Incorrect: The word "agua" is not masculine.

    D. Incorrect: The word "agua" is feminine and it should be "La".

    Answer B. Correct: "El" is used although the word "agua" is feminine.

    "Agua" is feminine but the masculine article is used due to the difficulty of saying "la agua". The vowels run together. To avoid this, the masculine article is used. However, "agua" retains its feminine gender. Therefore, any and all adjectives used need to agree in gender. "Pura" agrees in gender and number.

94. **A mí me gusta el chocolate, vino y cafe.**
    (Average Rigor)

    A. Correct: Words with natural emphasis on the second to last syllable do not require accent marks.

    B. Incorrect: Accents are required over the second to last syllable of "víno" and the last syllable of "café" to show emphasis.

    C. Incorrect: An accent is required on the last syllable of "café" for emphasis.

    D. Incorrect: Both words need accents on their last syllables, since each has an irregular emphasis on the last syllable.

    Answer C. Incorrect: "An accent is required on the last syllable of "café" for emphasis.

    Vino has a natural emphasis on the second to last syllable, so it does not require an accent mark. "Café" has an emphasis on the last syllable, requiring an accent mark.

95. **Necesito el informe para el lunes.**
    (Rigorous)

    A. Incorrect: "Para" is used to express a length of time.

    B. Correct: "Por" is used to express a length of time or specific hour.

    C. Incorrect: "Por" is used to indicate a specific deadline.

    D. Correct: "Para" is used to indicate a specific deadline.

    Answer D. "Para" is used to indicate a specific deadline.

    Only "para" can be used while speaking about deadlines or a specific time or day of week, making D the only suitable response. "Por" is used for general periods of time.

96. ¿Qué es la capital de Colombia?
    (Average Rigor)

    A. Correct: "Qué" is used to ask for a definition.

    B. Correct: "Qué" is used to elicit a choice between two or more items.

    C. Correct: "Qué" is used to elicit a choice.

    D. Incorrect: "Cuál" is used to imply a choice in the response.

    Answer D. Incorrect: "Cuál" is used to imply a choice in the response.

    "Cuál" must be used because it is the only one that is asking what the name of the capital of Colombia is. "Qué" is asking for what a capital is, i.e. the definition of a capital. "Cuál" signifies "which" and "Qué" signifies "what".

97. **Los médicos trabajan para el hospital.**
    (Rigorous)

    A. Correct: "Para" is used to indicate employed by.

    B. Incorrect: "Para" is used to designate the recipient of an action or destination.

    C. Incorrect: "Por" is used to indicate employed by.

    D. Incorrect: "Por" is used to express occupations.

    Answer A. Correct: "Para" is used to indicate employed by.

    "Para" must be used in this case to indicate that they are employed *by* the hospital. If "por" is used, it would imply that they are volunteers *of* the hospital. "Para" here translates as "for" while "por" would translate more as "because of".

98. ¿Quieres ir al cine conmigo? No quiero ir contigo.
    (Average Rigor)

    A. Incorrect: Spanish often requires a multiple, or double negative construction.

    B. Incorrect: The subjunctive is used to express a wish, desire or emotion.

    C. Correct: "No" precedes the verb.

    D. Incorrect: The direct object can be used at the end of an infinitive.

Answer A. Incorrect: Spanish often requires a multiple, or double, negative construction.

The correct answer is A since in Spanish, unlike English, a double negative construction is needed. The correct response would be "No, no quiero ir contigo". The subjunctive is not necessary, and the direct object cannot be used at the end of "ir" since the preposition "con" or "with" is being used.

TEACHER CERTIFICATION STUDY GUIDE

CULTURAL PERSPECTIVES

Choose the appropriate answer to complete the following items:

99. José Martí (1853-1895), era de ___.
    (Average Rigor)

    A.   México

    B.   Chile

    C.   Cuba

    D.   Argentina

    Answer C. Cuba.

    José Martí was born in Cuba and fought for Cuban independence through his writings until his death in 1895. He died just short of seeing Cuban independence and is a national hero of Cuba.

100. En 1971, Pablo Neruda (1904-1973) recibió el Premio Nóbel de ___.
    (Average Rigor)

    A.   Literatura

    B.   Arte

    C.   Ciencia

    D.   la Paz

    Answer A. Literatura

    Pablo Neruda, a renowned Chilean poet and writer, won the Nobel Prize in Literature in 1971 for his writings on Latin American society.

TEACHER CERTIFICATION STUDY GUIDE

101. Machu Picchu en el Perú es la antigua ciudad sagrada de los ___.
    (Easy)

    A. mayas

    B. incas

    C. aztecas

    D. olmecas

    Answer B. incas

    The Olmecas and Aztecs were located in what is today known as México. The Mayans were located throughout today's México and Central America. Answer B is correct because the Incas were in what is known as Perú today. Incan ancient ruins can be seen by visitors to Perú.

102. Miguel de Cervantes Saavedra mostró el conflicto entre _____ en "Don Quixote".
    (Rigorous)

    A. realismo y surrealismo

    B. sátira y humor

    C. idealismo y materialismo

    D. el campo y la ciudad

    Answer C. idealismo y materialismo

    Miguel de Cervantes Saavedra's character of Don Quixote was completely idealistic and removed from the harsh realities of the material world. He lived in an idealistic fantasy world, seeing the other characters in the novel as ideal characters instead of the people they were.

103. **Nicaragua está situada entre _____.**
    (Rigorous)

    A. Honduras y Costa Rica

    B. Costa Rica y Panamá

    C. Guatemala y El Salvador

    D. Guatemala y Belice

    Answer A. Honduras y Costa Rica

    Nicaragua is located in Central America bordered by Honduras to the north and Costa Rica to the south.

104. **El conquistador Hernán Cortés se encontró con el pueblo azteca y ___.**
    (Average Rigor)

    A. lo ayudó

    B. le proporcionó armas

    C. le enseñó a cultivar la tierra

    D. derrotó el imperio que el pueblo había creado

    Answer D. derrotó el imperio que el pueblo había creado

    Hernán Cortés was a conquistador and explorer who traveled from Spain to "The New World" in order to colonize their land and exploit natural resources. Cortés was horrified by the Aztecs' practice of human sacrifice, and attempting to put an end to it, killed many of the native Aztecs. Many native peoples also died from communicable diseases brought by the European colonists. In this way, the Aztec Empire was completely defeated.

105. Sor Juana Inés de la Cruz (1651-1695) era _____ mexicana.
    (Rigorous)

    A. una artista

    B. una muralista

    C. una poetisa y ensayista

    D. una novelista

    Answer C. una poetisa y ensayista

    To avoid being constrained by marriage, Sor Juana decided to become a nun to develop her studies and writings.

106. El pintor, Pablo Picasso, creó el estilo de arte llamado ___.
    (Average Rigor)

    A. surrealismo

    B. cubismo

    C. impresionismo

    D. realismo

    Answer B. cubismo

    Pablo Picasso, one of the most famous painters of all time, revolutionized the art world with his abstract paintings, creating a style known as "cubism".

107. ___ ocurrió 1936-1939.
 (Average Rigor)

   A. La Primera Guerra Mundial

   B. La Segunda Guerra Mundial

   C. La Guerra de Independencia de los Estados Unidos

   D. La Guerra Civil Española

   Answer D. La Guerra Civil Española

   The First World War was in 1917 and the second occurred in 1939. The United States declared its independence in 1776. The Spanish Civil War ushered in an era of fascism in Spain under Franco.

108. El "TLC" se refiere al ___.
 (Rigorous)

   A. Tratado comercial entre los EEUU, Canadá y México (Tratado de Libre Comercio)

   B. Tratado del 16 de septiembre

   C. Tratado de Guadalupe Hidalgo

   D. Tratado Liberal Cubano

   Answer A. Tratado comercial entre los EEUU, Canadá y México.

   The first Free Trade Agreement (Tratado de Libre Comercio) occurred between the United Status, Canada and Mexico.

109. Tenochtitlán era la capital de los ___.
     (Average Rigor)

   A. aztecas

   B. mayas

   C. zapotecas

   D. incas

   Answer A. aztecas

   The ancient capital of the Aztec people was Tenochtitlán. The capital city of Tenochtitlán, along with the entire Aztec empire, was destroyed by the Spanish conquerors.

110. Diego Rivera era ___.
     (Average Rigor)

   A. un novelista mexicano

   B. un pintor español del período surrealista

   C. un pintor mexicano del período surrealista

   D. un muralista cubano del período surrealista

   Answer C. un pintor mexicano del período surrealista

   Diego Rivera was a very famous Mexican painter during the surrealist era known for his large murals, his political activism for the Communist party, and his marriage to Frida Kahlo.

111. Simón Bolívar fue el primer presidente de ___, entre 1824 y 1826.
 (Rigorous)

    A. Perú

    B. Ecuador

    C. Chile

    D. Venezuela

Answer A. Perú

Simón Bolívar (1783-1830), from Venezuela, was an instrumental leader in many of Latin America's independence movements to oust Spain from its colonial territories. Bolívar was president of then Colombia (or Gran Colombia), Perú and Bolivia after their independence. The country of Bolivia was named after Bolívar.

112. El autor de "Cien años de soledad" es ___.
 (Average Rigor)

    A. Federico García Lorca

    B. Gabriel García Márquez

    C. Salvador Allende

    D. Octavio Paz

Answer B. Gabriel García Márquez

The Colombian author, Gabriel García Márquez, wrote the classic and world-renowned novel "*Cien años de soledad"* in addition to many others. Márquez is known for creating the literary style "realismo mágico" and won the Nobel Prize for Literature.

113. ___, el cantante de ópera, nació en México de padres españoles.
     (Easy)

  A. Diego Rivera

  B. Julio Iglesias

  C. Luis Miguel

  D. Plácido Domingo

Answer D. Plácido Domingo

Plácido Domingo is a famous opera singer, most well known for being one of "The Three Tenors" singing alongside Luciano Pavarotti and José Carreras.

114. **El gran artista "El Greco," nació en ___.**
     (Average Rigor)

  A. Creta

  B. Grecia continental

  C. Cerdeña

  D. Toledo

Answer A. Creta

El Greco", the renowned Spanish artist, was born in Crete. Although Crete was, at that time, part of the Republic of Venice in what is today, Italy; historically, Crete has been considered part of Greece and remains so today. Crete is an island off the mainland of Greece.

115. Andalucía, Cataluña, Galicia y Extremadura son ___.
    (Average Rigor)

    A.   ciudades españolas

    B.   ciudades latinoamericanas

    C.   comunidades autónomas de España

    D.   provincias latinoamericanas

    Answer C. comunidades autónomas de España

    Andalucía, Cataluña, Galicia y Extremadura are all considered "Autonomous Communities" encompassing one or more provinces in Spain. Each region of Spain is known for its own unique cultural and linguistic variations.

116. El colonialismo tuvo como objetivos principales, ___.
    (Rigorous)

    A.   beneficiarse de la desarrollada civilización de algunos pueblos indígenas

    B.   agotar los recursos naturales de los países conquistados

    C.   convertir los nativos al cristianismo y enseñarlos a luchar

    D.   extender el poder y el dominio de los países conquistadores a través de su imperio económico, político y religioso

    Answer D. extender el poder y el dominio de los países conquistadores a través de su imperio económico, político y religioso

    The purposes of colonialism included economic exploitation of the colony's natural resources, creation of new markets for the colonizer, and extension of the colonizer's way of life beyond its national borders. At that time, religious control was considered another form of power and unity with the mother country.

TEACHER CERTIFICATION STUDY GUIDE

117. Al recibir una invitación a cenar en España, usted debe preguntar ___.
(Average Rigor)

    A.   ¿Qué va a servir?

    B.   ¿A qué hora queréis que llegue?

    C.   ¿A qué hora me quieres llegar?

    D.   ¿Qué debo llevar?

Answer B. ¿A qué hora queréis que llegue?

This answer is grammatically correct because it uses the "vosotros" form, which is used primarily in Spain.

118. El Salvador, como muchos países en América Central, produce ___.
(Rigorous)

    A.   café y azúcar

    B.   café y bananas

    C.   azúcar y bananas

    D.   maíz y bananas

Answer A. café y azúcar

Although many countries in Central America depend on coffee, sugar and bananas as their principal agricultural products, El Salvador's main crops are coffee and sugar.

119. Por lo general, en los países latinoamericanos, se usa el tuteo para hablar con ___.
    (Easy)

    A. profesores y agentes de policía

    B. abogados, médicos y enfermeros

    C. amigos y miembros de la familia

    D. negociantes y empleados de tiendas

    Answer C. amigos y miembros de la familia

    "Tuteo" is the informal subject pronoun, "tú", which is the familiar "you" singular form used to talk to friends and family, rather than the formal, "usted" or the informal, plural "you all" "vosotros".

120. La ganadora del Premio Nóbel de Literatura, Gabriela Mistral, fue la primera mujer _____.
    (Rigorous)

    A. que ganó el Premio

    B. escritora de España

    C. escritora de América Latina

    D. escritora de lengua indígena

    Answer C. escritora de América Latina

    Gabriela Mistral was a famous writer and poet from Chile who won the Nobel Prize in Literature in 1945. She was the first female Latin American poet to win the award.

121. La mayoría de la música de Latinoamérica es una mezcla de los ritmos ____.
    (Rigorous)

    A. españoles y africanos

    B. españoles y nativos

    C. africanos y nativos

    D. mexicanos y españoles

    Answer C. africanos y nativos

    Due to colonialism and what came from colonialism (such as intermarriage and the intermixing of cultures, slavery and the forcible transport of Africans and therefore African culture to the colonies) the music of Latin America and the Hispanic world derives much of its music and musical rhythms from African and native cultures.

122. Se puede encontrar el uso muy frecuente del tuteo en ___.
    (Average Rigor)

    A. Argentina y Uruguay

    B. Chile, Cuba, Colombia y la mayoría de los países latinoamericanos

    C. sólo en España

    D. sólo en el Caribe

    Answer B. Chile, Cuba y Colombia y la mayoría de los países latinoamericanos

    The informal singular "tuteo" or "tú" form is used not only in Spain, it is frequently used in all Spanish-speaking countries as well. The "tú" form is the preferred form used in Chile, Cuba, Colombia and most countries of Latin America.

123. Barcelona es la capital de _____.
    (Average Rigor)

    A. España

    B. Valencia

    C. Andalucia

    D. Cataluña

    Answer D. Cataluña

    Spain is divided into regions, or provinces. While Madrid is the capital of the entire country of Spain, Barcelona is the capital of the province of Cataluña.

124. **Se usa el pronombre "vos" en ___.**
    (Average Rigor)

    A. España solamente

    B. lecturas y discursos

    C. Argentina, Perú, Chile, Ecuador y en otros países hispanos

    D. antiguas obras literarias

    Answer C. Argentina, Perú, Chile, Ecuador y en otros países hispanos

    There are regions in South America that use "vos" such as in the Southern Cone of Latin America. Other regions of northern South America will use "vos" as the preferred "you" construction.

125. Termine el dicho: "Dime con quién andas y ___."
 (Average Rigor)

   A. déjala correr

   B. mona se queda

   C. se lo pondrá

   D. te diré quién eres

Answer D. te diré quién eres

This is an idiomatic expression in the Spanish language. Literally translated it says, "Tell me with whom you are walking and I will tell you who you are". This really means, much like the English-language expression, "You can always tell a person by the company he keeps". In other words, the kind of people someone has as friends reflects on the kind of person s/he is.

INSTRUCTION AND ASSESSMENT

Complete the following statements about foreign language teaching methodology.

126. Krashen's Language Acquisition Theory contends that learning and acquisition of language are two distinct processes, with learning being ___.
     (Rigorous)

    A. the natural development of language as seen in children learning their native language

    B. the acquiring of language by the unconscious used in conversation

    C. a censor in one's mind that filters the correct and incorrect language

    D. formal and intentional knowledge about a language

    Answer D. formal and intentional knowledge about a language

    Answer D is correct since the learning portion of the Language Acquisition Theory states that learning is the deliberate undertaking of becoming knowledgeable about a language through being taught formally (grammar, structure, etc.). Answer A refers to natural order, Answer B refers to acquisition and Answer C refers to a monitor.

127. The five stages of Cultural Adaptation, or Culture Shock, are ___.
(Rigorous)

    A. Honeymoon, Disintegration, Re-integration, Autonomy, and Independence

    B. Fear, Coping, Rejection, Acquisition, and Learning

    C. Independence, Autonomy, Disintegration, Re-integration, and Fluency

    D. Inability to communicate, Frustration, Adaptation, Learning and Fluency

Answer A. Honeymoon, Disintegration, Re-integration, Autonomy, and Independence

Answer A is correct. These are the five stages of Cultural Adaptation, or Culture Shock that a person confronts when adapting to, not only a different language, but to the distinct culture that accompanies it.

128. A linguistic theory that sees language as the understanding and use of "linguistic units" within sentences aptly describes ___.
(Rigorous)

    A. the Theory of Discourse Analysis

    B. Pragmatics

    C. the Audio-lingual Approach

    D. Informal and Off-Hand technique

Answer A. the Theory of Discourse Analysis

Answer A. The Theory of Discourse Analysis treats language as linguistic units that are labeled, used and understood in speech. Answer B, Pragmatics is not correct since Pragmatics identifies the difference between the literal translation of what a speaker says versus the idea, or gist, that the speaker is trying to convey. Answer C, the Audio-lingual Approach is incorrect because this approach focuses on intensive memorization and in-class drills. Answer D, the Informal and Off-Hand technique are incorrect since they deal primarily with bringing cultural significance and cultural media into the act of learning language.

129. Content-based teaching, also known as the use of authentic materials, consists of ___.
(Rigorous)

- A. the tactile use of authentic cultural objects to reinforce language memory

- B. utilizing texts (passages, novels, articles) from authentic sources within the language. For example, reading a newspaper from Spain

- C. utilizing native speakers in the classroom to converse in, and clarify the language

- D. having the instructor choose, or allowing students to choose subjects that the students have genuine interest in; thereby, encouraging student analysis of these subjects

Answer D. having the instructor choose, or allowing students to choose subjects that the students have genuine interest in; thereby, encouraging student analysis of these subjects.

The core of content-based teaching is to make the content of the language being taught interesting to the students in the class in order to encourage learning. Answer A is not a defined method from the text. Answer B refers to the Informal and Off-hand technique, and Answer C refers to the technique known as having "the presence of another language's native speaker" present.

Choose the item which best describes the following:

130. Language is a set of habits, requiring oral practice of pattern drills and memorized responses. _____
    (Rigorous)

    A.   Grammatical Method

    B.   Audio-lingual Method

    C.   Natural Approach

    D.   Total Physical Response

    Answer B. Audio-lingual Method

    This is the standard definition for the Audio-lingual Method, which includes learning a language based on oral exercises and memorization to train the mind to memorize the language.

131. The emphasis is on communicative competence rather than memorizing grammar rules and stressing accuracy. _____
    (Rigorous)

    A.   Grammatical Method

    B.   Audio-lingual Method

    C.   Natural Approach

    D.   Total Physical Response

    Answer C. Natural Approach

    The Natural Approach to learning language teaches the acquisition of language through immersion in the language and an importance on communicating the message in the language first and worrying about grammar and structure later on in the language learning process.

132. This was originally used to teach Greek and Latin. Students learn elaborate grammar rules and bilingual lists of words. _____
    (Rigorous)

    A.   Grammatical Method

    B.   Audio-lingual Method

    C.   Natural Approach

    D.   Total Physical Response

    Answer A. Grammatical Method

    The Grammatical Method was used to teach the classical languages in a manner of accuracy and precision by focusing on grammar and structure, often through translation exercises.

133. This makes use of oral commands; students demonstrate their omprehension by physically reacting to the content of the message. _____
    (Rigorous)

    A.   Grammatical Method

    B.   Audio-lingual Method

    C.   Natural Approach

    D.   Total Physical Response

    Answer D. Total Physical Response

    The Total Physical Response method for language is much the way it sounds. This method utilizes the way in which a student naturally and physically comprehends the message by his or her physical behavior and response to what is being said. For example, the teacher says "sit" in the foreign language and the student reacts by sitting.

TEACHER CERTIFICATION STUDY GUIDE

READING COMPREHENSION
Read the short passages below and then choose the most accurate response based on your reading.

FEDERICO GARCÍA LORCA

El famoso poeta español, Federico García Lorca fue asesinado durante la Guerra Civil Española. Fue uno de los miembros más distinguidos de la generación llamada del 27. Su muerte fue trágica para el mundo entero.

García Lorca nació en Fuente Vaqueros en Granada el 5 de junio de 1898. Cuando era joven asistió en "la Facultad de Filosofía y Letras" en la ciudad de Córdoba. Pero un poco después, fue a Madrid para seguir sus estudios. Allí conoció a Pablo Picasso, a Salvador Dalí, a Manuel de Falla y a Andrés Segovia. Durante su vida tuvo la oportunidad de pintar, tocar la guitarra, escribir y viajar a Argentina, Cuba y los Estados Unidos.

Desafortunadamente, murió bajo misteriosas circunstancias el 19 de agosto, 1936; pero, su espíritu y talento viven hoy a través de su poesía y sus obras de teatro. Su muerte fue una pérdida profunda.

134. **García Lorca estudió en universidades en ___.**
    (Easy)

    A. Córdoba y Madrid

    B. Granada, Córdoba y Madrid

    C. Granada y Córdoba

    D. Argentina, Cuba, y los Estados Unidos

    Answer A. Córdoba y Madrid

    García Lorca studied in Córdoba and Madrid, Spain. With his many talents he was afforded the opportunity to travel to Argentina, Cuba and the United States.

135. Se hizo amigo de Picasso, Dalí, de Falla y Segovia en ____.
 (Easy)

 A. Granada

 B. Córdoba

 C. Fuente Vaqueros

 D. Madrid

 Answer D. Madrid

 When García Lorca left Córdoba to study in Madrid, he met Picasso, Dalí, de Falla and Segovia.

136. La idea principal de este pasaje es que García Lorca ____.
 (Average Rigor)

 A. viajó mucho

 B. murió muy joven

 C. fue un escritor con mucho talento y un futuro prometedor

 D. tenía muchos amigos

 Answer C. fue un escritor con mucho talento y un futuro prometedor

 Although García Lorca did die at a young age, the author's central theme focuses on the loss of literary talent for the nation. The other options are merely supporting facts about García Lorca's life.

137. Cuando murió, García Lorca tenía ____.
    (Easy)

    A.   27 años

    B.   36 años

    C.   38 años

    D.   49 años

    Answer C. 38 años

    García Lorca was 38 when he died. He was born in 1898 and died in 1936.

TEACHER CERTIFICATION STUDY GUIDE

LA TRAVESÍA DE LA TORMENTA

Hoy por la mañana, los investigadores del Centro Urbano predijeron que la tormenta se alejaría de la costa, aunque cientos de miles de habitantes huyeron de las playas e islas costeras, causando un frenético embrollo. Esta tarde, su trayectoria sigue alejándose de la región. La tormenta tenía más de 200 millas de ancho y vientos de 110 millas por hora.

138. ¿Todavía hay una amenaza en la costa?
 (Rigorous)

    A.   Si, hay un frenético embrollo.

    B.   Si, la tormenta está atravesándola.

    C.   No, las playas están lejanas.

    D.   No, la tormenta se alejó del área.

Answer D. No, la tormenta se alejó del área.

Although many people have left the beaches in a frenzy, the storm has backed away from the coast and is winding down.

139. ¿De qué tipo de fenómeno meteorológico trata la lectura?
 (Average Rigor)

    A.   Un terremoto

    B.   Una llovizna

    C.   Un tornado

    D.   Un huracán

Answer D. Un huracán

Although the text does not explicitly state that it is a hurricane, the characteristics of the storm described by the passage, lead the reader to believe it is a hurricane. Therefore, D is the most appropriate answer.

140. ¿Por qué huyó la gente?
    (Rigorous)

    A. Para estar a salvo

    B. Para ser vulnerable

    C. Para volver a casa

    D. Para ser atravesados por la tormenta

    Answer A. Para estar a salvo

    In spite of the fact that the storm was ending, coastal residents left their homes to be safe.

TEACHER CERTIFICATION STUDY GUIDE

Additional titles you may be interested in:

NES High School Mathematics 304

Prepare for your test with this state-aligned guide that reviews all of the current competency areas including: Mathematical Processes and Number Sense; Patterns, Algebra, and Functions; Measurement and Geometry; Trigonometry and Calculus; Statistics, Probability, and Discrete Mathematics. 16 competencies. 73 skills. Sample test has 150 questions.

ORELA Multiple-Subjects 001, 002, 003

Prepare for your test with this state-aligned guide that reviews all of the current competency areas including: Language Arts; Social Science; The Arts; Reading Instruction; Mathematics; Science; Health and Physical Education. 37 competencies. 187 skills. 30-question elementary education diagnostic test in book. Full 152-question sample test & 4 essays offered online.

ORELA Protecting Students and Civil Rights in the Educational Environment

From understanding federal and state laws that protect individual civil rights to the implications of student diversity for teaching and learning, this comprehensive guide covers all the core competencies within the two subareas of legal foundations and equity in the school environment. Test your knowledge with 60 sample questions.

Find out about the latest products and promotions.

300+ titles • FREE diagnostic tests • Study and test tips • Additional resources

www.ingramcontent.com/pod-product-compliance
Lightning Source LLC
Chambersburg PA
CBHW080536300426
44111CB00017B/2754